# WAR IN VIETNAM

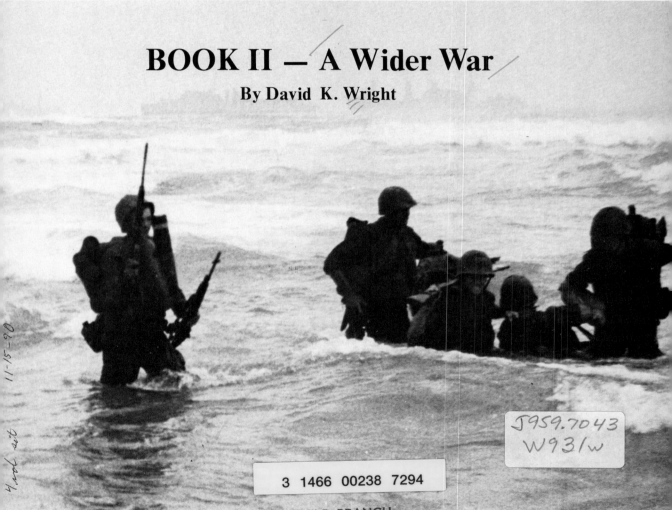

## BOOK II — A Wider War

By David K. Wright

CHILDRENS PRESS ®

CHICAGO

Library of Congress Cataloging-in-Publication Data

Wright, David K.
  War in Vietnam. (A wider war) / by David K. Wright.
    p.    cm.
  Includes index.
  Summary: Second of a four-book series, this volume
discusses the Vietnam War from 1965 to the Tet
Offensive in 1968.
  ISBN 0-516-02287-3
  1.  Vietnamese Conflict, 1961-1975—Juvenile
literature.  [1.  Vietnamese Conflict, 1961-
1975.]  I.  Title.  II.  Title: Wider war.
DS557.7.W75   1988                         88-14919
959.704′3—dc19                             CIP
                                           AC

Childrens Press®, Chicago

# Contents

# Foreword

Vietnam. The land, the war, the experience continue to haunt the nation. It was the first war America lost, and lost causes always seem to leave more questions than answers. The four-volume series *War in Vietnam* by David K. Wright looks at why the United States became involved, why we fought the war the way we did, and why we lost. In seeking answers to these questions, Mr. Wright contributes to the healing of the nation, which remains the unfinished business of the war.

In Book I—*Eve of Battle*, Wright describes the early history of Vietnam up to the critical year 1965, when the first U. S. combat troops arrived in South Vietnam. We learn of Vietnam's long tradition of fierce independence, the period of French rule over the country, the first French-Indochina war involving the nationalist Viet Minh, and the growing American involvement following the French defeat in 1954. Wright shows us how America's entanglement deepened step by step. By 1965 the leaders in Washington, D. C., felt they had no choice but to send U. S. combat troops to save Vietnam from communism. *Eve of Battle* reveals the danger of making important national decisions without really understanding the nature and history of the people we have pledged to support.

Book II—*A Wider War* explores one of the most puzzling questions of the conflict. Why couldn't the United States—the world's greatest military power—defeat a poorly equipped peasant army? Some argue that America's politicians would not use the military force necessary to win. But *A Wider War* shows that the amount of force Americans used was much greater than in any other war. Such firepower and violence—from the smallest infantry unit to the giant B-52 bombers—turned the Vietnamese peasants against the U. S. It turned many Americans against the war as well. To these people, including some Vietnam veterans, it appeared that time was on the enemy's side. Before long, many in America lost patience with this long, costly, and savage war.

Book III—*Vietnamization* tells of the events that followed the 1968 election of Richard Nixon as President. Even though Nixon had pledged to seek "peace with honor," he pursued a complex and at times dishonest policy in running the war. In violation of the law, Nixon ordered U.S. troops to invade Cambodia and Laos. We also learn how he promised to reduce the number of U. S. troops in Vietnam yet still increase support for the South Vietnamese Army. He stepped up the bombing of North Vietnam at the same time he began secret talks with the enemy in Paris. This book also wrestles with the agonizing question of how American soldiers could have taken part in the March 1968 massacre of innocent Vietnamese civilians. The My Lai 4 incident, in which hundreds of men, women, and children were murdered, remains a black mark against America's honor. The book concludes with the heavy Christmas bombing of North Vietnam in December 1972 and with the January 1973 cease-fire agreement. The treaty ended American involvement in Vietnam but did not end the war.

The final book—*The Fall of Vietnam*—recounts the tragic consequences of America's confused policies in Vietnam. In our efforts to bring democracy and freedom to this far-away nation, we nearly lost sight of these values at home. The Watergate political scandal showed that even President Nixon and his close advisers were willing to break the law to stay in power. Richard Nixon became the only President in history forced to resign in disgrace. In one sense he can be counted as a victim of Vietnam. More tragic victims were the populations of North and South Vietnam, Cambodia, and Laos. Many U. S. Vietnam veterans also remain troubled victims of the war. No one can predict when the agony will end for the families of MIAs—those reported missing in action from 1965 to 1973. These families have waited for years to hear some word about the fate of their loved ones.

Vietnam is a sad chapter in the nation's history. The series *War in Vietnam* will help readers find answers to many of their questions about the war. The biggest question of all may be—Was Vietnam an isolated, regrettable event, or did our conduct of the war reveal the darker side of the American character? The answer to this question, perhaps more than any other, has meaning for the nation's future.

Frank A. Burdick
*Professor of History at*
*State University College*
*Cortland, New York*

# A Vietnam Timeline: Major Events in A Wider War

## 1965

February 7: Viet Cong attack U.S. bases. President Johnson replies to the attacks by bombing targets in North Vietnam.

March 8: The first American combat soldiers— 3,500 Marines— arrive in Vietnam to guard Danang airbase.

March 24: Antiwar teach-in is held at the University of Michigan in Ann Arbor. Teach-ins take place throughout 1965 on many college and university campuses.

April: North Vietnamese prepare the first launching pad for Russian surface-to-air (SAM) missiles.

May 15: National antiwar teach-in held in Washington, D.C.

May 24: First U.S. Army division leaves U.S. for Vietnam.

June 11: Air Force General Nguyen Cao Ky takes over as South Vietnam's prime minister.

July 28: General William Westmoreland, commander of American forces in

President Lyndon B. Johnson

8

Vietnam, asks for and gets an increase in U.S. troops.

**October through mid-November:** U.S. Army soldiers defeat North Vietnamese Army (NVA) troops in the first major battle between American and North Vietnamese forces. The fighting takes place in the remote Ia Drang valley.

**December 25:** U.S. bombing of North Vietnam is suspended by President Lyndon B. Johnson, who hopes the North Vietnamese will meet with him to talk peace.

**December 31:** U.S. troop strength in Vietnam numbers 200,000.

## 1966

**January 31:** President Johnson orders the bombing of North Vietnam to resume.

**January-February:** The Senate Foreign Relations Committee questions President Johnson's advisers about U.S. involvement in the war.

**February 8:** President Johnson and South

Vietnamese children.

Vietnamese leaders call for peace following a meeting in Hawaii.

March 10: Buddhists demonstrate against the South Vietnamese government. Ky responds by using troops to quell demonstrations.

April 12: B-52 bombers are used for the first time in air raids against North Vietnam.

December: North Vietnamese leaders meet and agree to fight the war with both troops and diplomacy.

## 1967

January: North Vietnam says that the U.S. must stop its air raids before peace talks can begin.

January: Operation Cedar Falls begins. This massive military action is designed to rid the Iron Triangle near Saigon of enemy soldiers. Villages believed sympathetic to the Viet Cong are levelled and the people relocated to refugee camps.

Jungle warfare.

| | |
|---|---|
| February 22: | Operation Junction City begins. A plan to trap Viet Cong in a jungle area northwest of Saigon, the operation results in few VC captured despite five major battles. |
| April 28: | General William Westmoreland addresses Congress on the war in Vietnam, asking for greater support. |
| July: | The North Vietnamese meet to plan a "Great Uprising" in 1968 in the South. The uprising became known as the Tet Offensive. |
| August: | Secretary of Defense Robert McNamara meets behind closed doors with U.S. senators. He informs them that the saturation bombing of North Vietnam is not weakening North Vietnamese will to fight. |
| September 3: | General Nguyan Van Thieu is elected president of South Vietnam. |
| November: | U.S. Marines occupy Khe Sanh, a hilltop near the border of Laos. They are soon surrounded by over 35,000 NVA soldiers. |

General William Westmoreland.

| | |
|---|---|
| December 31: | The number of U.S. troops in Vietnam reaches nearly 500,000. |

## 1968

| | |
|---|---|
| January 30-31: | The Tet Offensive begins as Viet Cong and North Vietnamese troops attack most major cities in South Vietnam and major American military bases. |
| February 25: | U.S. and South Vietnamese forces, after weeks of fierce fighting, retake the city of Hué, ending the Tet Offensive. |

# Chapter 1

# Fateful Decisions

Two events dominated the 1960s for the United States. One was the assassination of U.S. President John F. Kennedy on November 22, 1963. The other was the Vietnam War, which began for America in 1965 and ended in failure eight years later. If you focus on either event, President Lyndon Baines Johnson (LBJ) commands your attention.

Neither Johnson nor anyone else expressed a great deal of surprise when South Vietnam's corrupt President Diem was assassinated on November 1, 1963. Americans believed other countries often got rid of their leaders that way. They felt it could not happen here. Yet only three weeks later, the nation was stunned by the assassination of President Kennedy in Dallas. The young President was struck down by two bullets, apparently fired by sniper Lee Harvey Oswald. A few hours later, Vice President John-

son was sworn in as President.

Johnson had earned his way onto the Democratic ticket in 1960 by being a Texas moderate amid a group of eastern liberals. Feared and respected in the Senate, he was seen at first as a "caretaker" President, someone who would merely serve out Kennedy's term until the next election. But Johnson amazed everyone by introducing the most far-reaching social legislation in the nation's history. His Great Society programs helped create better jobs, better housing, and better educational opportunities for Americans. They also established equal rights for blacks and other Americans who had always been have-nots. Johnson's actions helped him achieve a landslide victory over Republican Senator Barry Goldwater in the 1964 presidential election.

The public agreed with Johnson that it was time to enforce equal

President Lyndon B. Johnson.

rights laws. They also voted for him because he pledged to keep U.S. soldiers out of the worsening conflict in Southeast Asia. By May 1965, an incredible 74 percent of the American people approved of the way Johnson was running the country. In his ability to deal with Congress and his vision for the nation, he may have been one of the greatest Presidents ever to hold office. He sent aid to flooded farms in the Midwest; he saved the lives of Americans caught in a Caribbean uprising; he soothed college students who resented the way huge universities were treating them. Yet these and other problems were gradually overshadowed by Vietnam.

This long, narrow country on the coast of Southeast Asia had been the scene of struggle for centuries. The Vietnamese spent more than 1,000 years fighting China. Once the Chinese were expelled, Europeans with modern weapons invaded. By 1887, France ruled the Indochina Union, made up of Vietnam, Laos, and Cambodia.* Japanese soldiers overran Vietnam, replacing the French in World War II. After the defeat of Japan in 1945,

the French returned a year later to resume control. They were not driven out of Vietnam until 1954, when they lost the battle of Dien Bien Phu to the Vietnamese.

Victory over the French created numerous problems for Vietnam. Without French trade and assistance, the Vietnamese economy began to fail. To make matters worse, the Vietnamese themselves were divided over how their country should be run. Many North Vietnamese believed the nation should be a communist state, headed by an elderly revolutionary leader named Ho Chi Minh. Many South Vietnamese wanted some form of capitalism. Most Vietnamese, however, were so concerned with simply earning a living that they did not have time for political opinions.

The Geneva Conference, held in 1954 in Geneva, Switzerland, formally ended the war between Vietnam and France. The peace agreement created two Vietnams, divided by a demilitarized zone at the 17th parallel. Free elections were to be held in 1956 to decide who should run a single, reunited country. When the time for elections arrived, South Vietnam

*After the Vietnam War, Cambodia's name was changed to Kampuchea. Because we cover events before 1975, we use the name Cambodia throughout.

14

Protest in the 1960s took some strange forms.

U.S. Marines depart a wet helicopter landing zone.

refused to hold them, fearing the communists would win. Communists who lived in the South, called Viet Cong (VC), began to attack government officials. While these guerrilla fighters bullied or killed mayors, police, and others, the North Vietnamese were trying to improve their economy. When the Viet Cong needed weapons and supplies, they turned to their allies in North Vietnam.

Meanwhile, South Vietnam's leaders asked their friends for aid, especially the United States. From the South Vietnamese viewpoint, the U.S. seemed the perfect choice. The country was rich and powerful, and Americans feared the spread of communism in any part of the world.

Vietnamese officials in Saigon made long lists of weapons, equipment, food, and building materi-

Some U.S. aid money went to educate the Vietnamese.

als they needed. American officials granted their requests—and sent civilian and military advisers as well. U.S. civilians taught South Vietnamese modern farming and construction techniques. U.S. military advisers taught the Vietnamese army how to fight the Viet Cong and often accompanied them on patrol.

When these tactics did not produce quick victories, President Johnson made the first in a series of fateful decisions that were to lead the nation deeper and deeper into the Vietnam conflict. General William Westmoreland, put in command of U.S. forces in Vietnam in 1964, urged the President to increase U.S. involvement in the war. In reply to enemy attacks on American military bases, Johnson ordered U.S. warplanes to bomb North Vietnamese targets in early 1965. He also decided to send U.S. soldiers to guard American bases in South Vietnam.

The first American combat soldiers in Vietnam arrived on March 8, 1965, when 3,500 Marines splashed ashore at Danang. The large airbase was located on the seacoast in the northern part of South Vietnam. The Marines were to guard the base against enemy infiltration and attack. A few weeks after setting up camp, they had cleared a wide area around the Danang base and made it safe from enemy fire.

The average Marine at that time probably saw himself as saving the Vietnamese people from the communists threatening their country. The average peasant probably did not know or care much for politics. To them, the Marines were simply the latest in a long line of foreign intruders.

Who was winning the war at this time? At first it looked as if the South Vietnamese could do the job on their own. With their U.S. advisers, they found and overpowered several Viet Cong units. Much of their early success, however, was due to the weather.

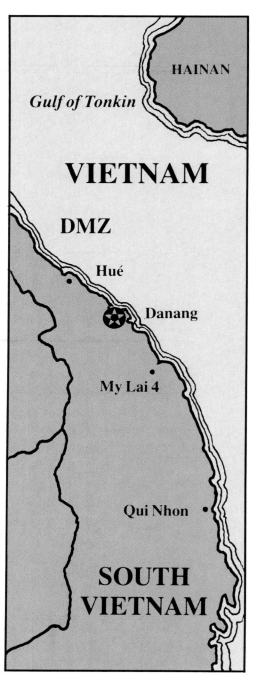

Danang was the site of a huge American airbase.

During the dry season, the Army of the Republic of Vietnam (ARVN) soldiers could make up in the air what strength they lacked on the ground. When they ran into the enemy, they called in artillery and air power. Helicopters raked Viet Cong and North Vietnamese positions with machine guns and small rockets, while fighter-bombers hammered the enemy. Then the rainy or monsoon season came with its torrential downpour. The weather grounded most planes, and the communists began to move.

As the fighting continued, greater numbers of North Vietnamese Army (NVA) soldiers began coming south along the Ho Chi Minh Trail. The trail began in North Vietnam, curved westward into Laos, and ran as far south as Cambodia. An asphalt highway in some places and a narrow ledge in others, the trail was bombed every day by U.S. planes. The enemy began traveling at night and hiding trucks and supplies in the thick jungle. In this way they were able to move thousands of men and tons of weapons and food south. The buildup was noticed along the Vietnam-Laos

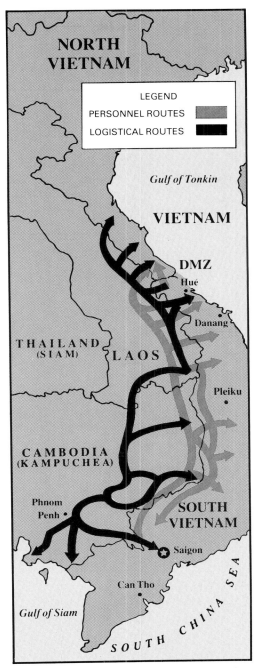

The Ho Chi Minh Trail wound through three countries.

border, where a string of native villages contained a few U.S. Army Special Forces soldiers.

These Green Berets, as they were known, lived among the Montagnards, or mountain people, in South Vietnam. The mountain tribes were not true Vietnamese and disliked the lowland people in the North and South. When Special Forces teams treated the sick and taught the Montagnards to defend themselves, the people became pro-American. They led Green Berets along secret highlands trails. This allowed the Special Forces troops in each village to spy on enemy movement. Also eyeing the enemy were employees of America's Central Intelligence Agency (CIA). The CIA used space-age "people sniffers," or heat-sensing devices, and other equipment that showed a steady stream of soldiers and supplies pouring into South Vietnam.

Considering the aerial bombardment North Vietnam was taking, the stream was a miracle. Beginning in March 1965, U.S. Air Force and Navy jet bombers pounded North Vietnamese military targets. Wave after wave of

supersonic planes rocketed north, bombing to within 20 miles of the northern capital of Hanoi and the major port, Haiphong. President Johnson called the bombing Operation Rolling Thunder. It was a fitting name for the destruction that rained down on highways,

An American Navy pilot in North Vietnamese hands.

bridges, and factories. The North Vietnamese retaliated by shooting down many of the multimillion-dollar jets and taking U.S. pilots prisoner. As the number of prisoners grew, they were paraded before television cameras and appeared on the nightly news in the United States.

Americans watched in growing concern as the war escalated. Many citizens formed opinions that no longer supported the President and his policies.

On April 4, 1965, *The New York Times* carried a full-page ad

Antiwar sentiment angered President Johnson.

addressed to President Johnson. The ad included the names of 2,500 ministers, priests, and rabbis. The headline begged the President to stop the war. These citizens were not radicals but clergypeople who were aware that men, women, and children were dying every day in Asia.

An increasing number of college students began to see things the same way. A National Coordinating Committee to End the War in Vietnam began at the University of Wisconsin. Until the United States pulled out of Vietnam in 1973, this office kept antiwar groups informed of meetings, rallies, and other events throughout the country.

Occasionally, the debate over Vietnam had its humorous side. In one instance, University of Wisconsin students were returning from a 1965 antiwar rally in Washington, D.C. They were passed by a fellow student's car going the opposite way toward the nation's capital. The student was carrying a petition from 600 fellow students urging the President to continue the war!

The more people knew about Vietnam, the less many of them wanted the war to continue. One group in particular understood the situation in Vietnam as few did. These were members of the International Voluntary Services, who spoke Vietnamese and worked to improve the lives of villagers in Vietnam. The war, they said, made their work futile. While they could help a few families each day, the U.S. military was creating hundreds of refugees, many wounded, every day. How could anyone help people while they were being made homeless or wounded or killed, they asked. They wrote a letter of protest to the President, but it never reached LBJ. Many of the President's advisers who knew of the letter sharply criticized the volunteers' patriotism and knowledge of the situation.

In fact, many of Johnson's

### Dean Rusk

*Dean Rusk (born February 9, 1909), U.S. Secretary of State, 1961-1969, under presidents Kennedy, Johnson, and Nixon*

*Rusk was born into a poor family in rural Georgia. A brilliant student, Rusk worked his way through college, then went to England to study. After World War II, he joined the foreign service and served as Assistant Secretary of State for Far Eastern affairs during the Eisenhower administration.*

*Rusk and Lyndon Johnson wanted to send U.S. troops to Indochina in 1954 to help the French. While LBJ often had second thoughts about U.S. involvement in Vietnam, his Secretary of State remained a "hawk" to the end. He was impatient with the many poor governments of South Vietnam, but always believed that they were better than a communist takeover. Nevertheless, in 1965 Rusk wanted to explore all diplomatic possibilities before giving his approval to bombing raids in North Vietnam.*

*Rusk remained loyal to Johnson throughout LBJ's term as President. The Secretary of State even endorsed a policy known as "Vietnamization," the idea that the Vietnamese should do more of the fighting and the U.S. less of it.*

*In 1969, Rusk returned to Georgia to teach law, still convinced that the United States had upheld its beliefs in Vietnam.*

Thousands of young men were drafted and trained for Vietnam.

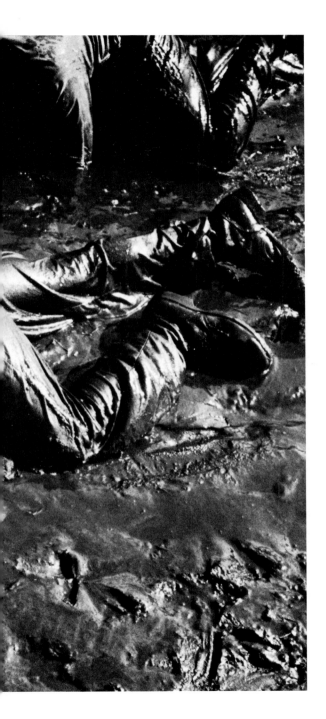

closest advisers were much more committed to the war than was the President himself. Secretary of State Dean Rusk, a lifelong foe of communism, and special adviser Walt Rostow were two of several strong prowar people in the administration. They argued in support of Westmoreland's requests for troops and arms. In public, LBJ lashed out at anyone who was opposed to the military buildup. In private, he had great misgivings. How could his Great Society programs work if tax money went to fund the war? It was true that orders for weapons caused defense plants to hire people, giving the public more money and helping the economy. But the U.S. military buildup had to be paid for with tax dollars.

Neither the war nor the huge increases in government spending were what President Johnson had had in mind when he was elected in 1964. By the summer of 1965, with 200,000 American soldiers in Vietnam, the war seemed out of control.

# Chapter 2

# Battles Large and Small

In the early years of the war, General William Westmoreland put American troops only in defensive positions in Vietnam. They were to protect aircraft, fuel depots, and fellow soldiers. This was called the enclave or fortress strategy. Chasing the enemy would be left to the Army of the Republic of Vietnam (ARVN).

Westmoreland quickly saw that this strategy would not help end the war. ARVN officers were not always competent leaders. They trapped the enemy, only to let them slip away. So the general asked for and received more U.S. troops. Among the thousands of soldiers sent to Vietnam was an entirely new kind of combat unit called the 1st Air Cavalry Division.

The cavalry riding to the rescue has always been a favorite image from the American West. The Army liked the cavalry so much that it did not retire the last horse until after World War II! The 1st

Cav, as it was known, combined an old idea with a new one. This 10,000-man unit's strength was mobility—moving quickly from one place to another. But instead of using horses, the Cav moved by air in helicopters that protected troops with machine guns and rockets. The helicopters let them fly into enemy territory, fight a battle, and as quickly fly out again. The chance to test this airborne cavalry came in November 1965 in a misty, jungle-filled area near the Cambodian border. The place was the Ia Drang River valley.

For months, Viet Cong and North Vietnamese Army (NVA) troops had controlled rural central Vietnam. In October 1965, they attacked a Special Forces camp at Plei Me. The 1st Cavalry chased the enemy westward, deep into the valley. Lone U.S. aircraft sent over the valley drew enemy fire, and the pilots relayed enemy positions. Within minutes 1st Cav

Army of the Republic of Vietnam (ARVN) troops

helicopters filled with troops were in the air. Often outnumbered, the cavalry units relied on surprise to give them an advantage while more troops were flown in. Terrible fighting, some of it hand-to-hand combat, continued night and day. For weeks, enemy troops, spotted from the air, were bombarded or chased and ambushed by U.S. airmobile soldiers.

Cavalry tactics, while effective, were not perfect. Several times, helicopter landing zones or LZs were "hot." This meant the men found themselves dropped into the middle of a large enemy force. These Cav soldiers could be shot to pieces minutes after the helicopters left. In many cases, artillery and air strikes prevented the Americans from being overrun. But other times the enemy was so close that planes or artillery fire were useless. Reinforcements sent to rescue soldiers pinned down by enemy fire had to watch for ambushes. The close-in fighting resulted in some American troops being hit by their own shells or bullets. By the end of November, after weeks of bitter skirmishes, enemy soldiers withdrew westward across the border into Cambodia.

The Ia Drang valley battles proved to be important for several reasons. North Vietnamese generals had wondered if their troops would run from American soldiers. In fact, they fought bravely. The NVA and Viet Cong lost 3,500 men, compared to 240 Americans reported dead. This showed that they were willing to take heavy losses in human life. U.S. soldier deaths and injuries, however, may not have been reported correctly in the early years of the war. That is because American officers were convinced that a favorable "kill ratio" (their dead versus our dead) was important. Numbers aside, any plan the enemy had had to divide South Vietnam by holding the Ia Drang valley had failed.

The battles also proved that the airmobile cavalry was a sound idea. After Ia Drang, the enemy returned to guerrilla fighting: hide and strike, hit and run. But cavalry soldiers could move in and out of the thick jungle where guerrilla fighters hid. They could drop amid the enemy and create confusion. The valley fighting also showed that the use of artillery

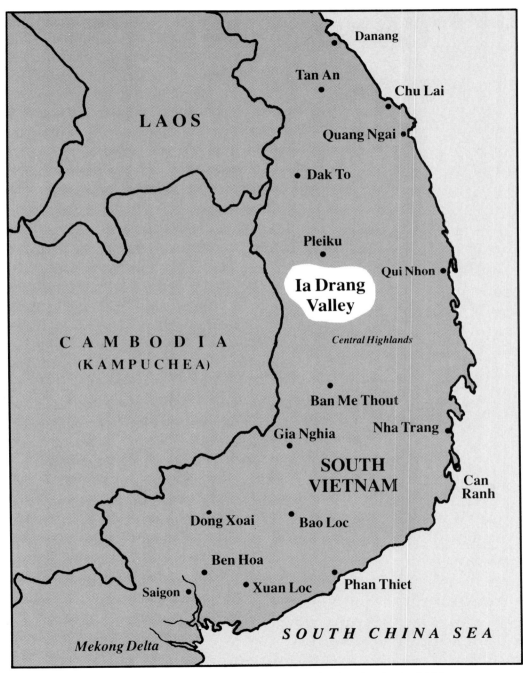

The remote Ia Drang Valley was a major battle site in 1965.

and B-52 bombers, though successful, had its limits. Such massive firepower could level acres of enemy territory and kill many VC and NVA. Yet artillery and air strikes were dangerous to use if the enemy got too close to friendly forces.

Other battles were taking place as America sent thousands of troops to Southeast Asia. One was named Operation Cedar Falls. It was created to chase the Viet Cong out of hiding places close to Saigon. For years the enemy had used marshes, thick forests, rubber plantations, and small villages near the Saigon River as hiding places. Clearing the area of the enemy would remove Saigon's constant fear of attack and make such major U.S. sites as Tan Son Nhut airbase more secure.

Cedar Falls was a search-and-destroy mission, which meant that the enemy would be hunted until found and then wiped out. It began on the morning of January 8, 1967. The area under attack, called the Iron Triangle, had been hammered with thousands of tons of bombs before the first U.S. soldier entered. Every square foot was a target for bombs and shells

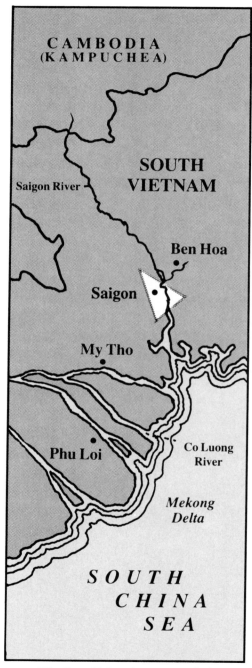

The Iron Triangle surrounded Saigon.

except one village—a tiny place called Ben Suc. According to the plan, the VC would try to seek refuge in the village and be trapped there.

When the bombing stopped, hundreds of American troops landed in Ben Suc, surprising local residents. The U.S. had hoped to surprise the VC, too. While the villagers turned out to be pro-Viet Cong, there were very few enemy soldiers found among them. The biggest operation launched so far by the United States in Vietnam had yielded only a handful of frightened villagers.

Several Vietnamese who may or may not have been enemy soldiers were killed. Ben Suc was then bulldozed and burned to the ground. Americans believed they could move villagers to a new site and remove the influence of the Viet Cong in that way. This angered the villagers, who were no longer able to farm their land. As one Army officer sadly remarked, "If they weren't VC when we showed up, they were VC by the time we left." He realized that it was important to deprive the enemy of this village, where they received food and

A wounded Viet Cong suspect

Viet Cong-built booby traps awaited careless Americans.

shelter. The officer also knew that destroying the village had made enemies of friend and foe alike.

But what had happened to the Viet Cong? According to all reports, they had been in the Iron Triangle a few hours before dawn on January 8. Shortly after Operation Cedar Falls ended, numerous Viet Cong were seen once again in the Iron Triangle. Where could they have gone?

The complete answer did not come until after the war, when Viet Cong soldiers showed reporters the incredible tunnel network they had dug in the area. These tunnels, which ran for miles a few feet below ground, saved the VC from destruction. Even though during the war the U.S. found 500 tunnels, some filled with rice, supplies, and enemy soldiers, this represented only a small fraction of the total tunnel area. The tunnels were checked by Army "tunnel rats," soldiers who bravely entered tiny earthen holes armed only with a pistol and a flashlight. Booby traps, snakes, insects, and enemy soldiers often awaited them. These tunnel mazes proved to be one of the decisive factors in the Vietnamese victory.

There were, of course, many other military operations. They came in all sizes. For example, the Marines chased two North Vietnamese Army divisions back across the demilitarized zone, the line separating North and South Vietnam. This was a huge operation, lasting more than two weeks in the summer of 1966. At the other extreme, a 1st Infantry Division operation involved finding a single sniper who shot at passing traffic from a small village.

From the soldier's point of view large operations had certain advantages. According to one infantryman, "We always felt the odds were better in a great big operation. It's tough to ambush a whole battalion [about 500 men]. Besides, in a big operation, the enemy always hid. I went on one operation that lasted two weeks. We didn't see one enemy soldier or hear one enemy rifle. That was OK."

The typical U.S. foot soldier was a member of a squad. There were six to ten members in the squad. Four squads made up a platoon. Four platoons of 25 to 40 men each made up a company. Four companies, 100 to 160 men each, made up a battalion. Four battalions made up a brigade that totaled 400 to 640 men each. Four brigades, with a total of 1,600 to 2,560 men, made up a division. Divisions had from 12,000 to 18,000 men. For every combat soldier there were several support personnel. These people in the division—supply specialists, clerks, cooks, medics—kept the fighters healthy, clothed, paid, and supplied in the field to battle the enemy.

Almost all U.S. soldiers in Vietnam wore lightweight nylon jungle fatigue clothing. These pants and shirts had big pockets. They were worn with socks and boots but often without underwear because of the heat. Too many layers of clothes could irritate the skin. The boots were black leather and olive nylon mesh. They had drain holes that helped keep feet dry. Soldiers also wore olive plastic helmet liners, which fit into olive-colored steel helmets. The liners and heavy helmets were sometimes left behind in favor of bandanas or beat-up, floppy jungle hats. Towels were sometimes worn around necks to soak up sweat and to keep straps holding heavy equipment from cutting into a man's shoulders.

Each soldier carried about 60 pounds of gear. Meals, called field rations, were hauled in small cardboard boxes. In the middle of nowhere, food was the highlight of the day. Inside each box was a can of bread; a can of fruit; and a can of ham and lima beans, beef stew, or some other main meal. Smaller tins contained peanut butter, jelly, or honey. Also in each box were matches, a pack of five cigarettes, plastic utensils, and toilet paper. Meals were heated in clever ways. A tiny chunk of a plastic explosive called C-4 was lighted and used as a cooking fire. Another method involved squirting a tin of peanut butter with insect repellent and setting it afire! Beer and soft drinks, carried warm in boot socks, often ended the meal.

Each man had one or two canteens of water, socks, a rain poncho, a short shovel for digging foxholes, plus hand grenades and ammunition. One man in each squad carried a larger gun, an M-60 machine gun. This weapon fired bullets linked together in

A U.S. soldier, carrying machine-gun ammunition, steps carefully over a log.

long belts. Several squad members had to carry belts of this machine-gun ammunition. Another squad member carried a stubby gun that fired grenades. This M-79 grenade launcher could shoot small explosives very accurately up to 300 yards.

Still another squad member hauled a radio on his back. Known as the radio-telephone operator, he stayed close to the squad leader, usually a sergeant. The platoon leader was a lieutenant, while a captain commanded the company. Everyone in the squad who did not carry an M-60 or M-79 carried an M-16 rifle. This weapon weighed about six pounds and fired small bullets either one at a time or automatically out of a metal box called a clip. With their machine guns, grenade launchers and rifles, a squad of Vietnam-era soldiers could produce more firepower than a platoon of World War II troops.

The Viet Cong, on the other hand, usually carried no more than a few pounds into battle. Their "uniform" was often black silk, pajama-like shirts and trousers and sandals. In some cases the sandals were made out

An electronically controlled anti-mortar device.

36

An infantry platoon could create immense firepower.

of pieces of car or truck tires! The North Vietnamese army had regular uniforms, and their battle kit items resembled those American troops carried.

The enemy's weapons were Soviet- or Chinese-made rifles, machine guns, grenades, and mortars, although they also captured many weapons from South Vietnamese troops and U.S. bases. Because they could hide food, ammunition, and other supplies in tunnels or villages, they did not need to carry much with them. They could travel faster and lighter than American or South Vietnamese troops and often could endure the heat and humidity better. Nevertheless, they did not have the firepower or troop numbers that U.S. and South Vietnamese forces could put into the field in any one place.

U.S. soldiers enjoyed a great many advantages over the enemy, but none as great as having artillery on their side. Artillery is a big gun that can fire shells for several miles. Americans often picked a spot in the middle of an operation to construct a fire base. This was an artillery base ringed with sandbag fortifications and stocked with several kinds of exploding shells. The most common artillery gun was the 105 mm howitzer, which could fire a shell at a target ten miles away. Four men worked each gun, with several howitzers at each fire base. Infantry troops guarded the base, because it was always a prime enemy target.

Artillery (and air strikes, for that matter) was called in by a forward observer or by some other leader sent out to find the enemy. The technique worked as follows: if the enemy was in a fortified position and artillery was needed, the forward observer used a map and a radio to tell the fire base where the enemy was located and what kinds of shells to use. Usually, the observer directed the artillery crew to fire behind the enemy, then told them how to adjust their guns to get the shells

closer to the enemy. This technique was known as "walking" shells toward the target. If Americans faced being overrun by enemy troops, artillery could be called in right on top of the U.S. position.

The fire base also had an 81 mm mortar. This weapon was a short tube propped up with a tripod on a big metal base. When a shell was dropped down the tube, it fired as it hit the bottom. Mortars weighed about 100 pounds and could be carried by three men. They had a range of about three miles.

In contrast to the lightweight mortars, there were huge artillery guns at permanent bases and even larger guns on battleships offshore. Both were used if heavy fighting took place anywhere near their positions.

When infantry units ran into fortified enemy positions, they sometimes used more precise weapons. One was the LAW (light antitank weapon). This was Vietnam's answer to the World War II bazooka. The LAW was a fiberglass tube with just one shell inside it. An aiming device and a trigger were attached to the tube. The weapon could be aimed and fired precisely at an enemy bunker. The tube was then thrown away.

While the Viet Cong and North Vietnamese could not match U.S. or South Vietnamese artillery strength, they made good use of their own mortars. Mortar attacks on airbases, infantry troops, villages, cities, convoys, and camps took their toll during the war. The cry "Incoming!" alerted everyone to an enemy mortar attack and sent troops scrambling for cover. North Vietnamese raids on U.S. and South Vietnamese ammunition dumps often kept enemy troops supplied in the

Helicopters allowed foot soldiers to land in hostile terrain.

A Vietnamese mother and child hide during a firefight.

field. As one U.S. sergeant remarked grimly, "We got every one of our stolen mortars back—one shell at a time."

Perhaps the greatest advantage on the North Vietnamese and VC side was their knowledge and use of the land and its people. Enemy troops knew the location of thousands of tunnels, swamps, rivers, villages, and other hiding places. They could camouflage themselves in the jungle or among the population. In the end, this advantage proved more effective than the sophisticated weapons and artillery of American and South Vietnamese forces.

The North Vietnamese and Viet Cong lost nearly every major battle against U.S and South Vietnamese troops, yet they continued to fight. Ho Chi Minh and Prime Minister Pham Van Dong showed no signs of calling for an end to the conflict nor of accepting the division of Vietnam. By the end of 1967, some American advisers and military commanders began to fear the war might last longer and cost a great deal more than the leaders in Washington realized.

# Chapter 3

# Hardships in a Strange War

No two soldiers had the same experience in Vietnam. One Army private could patrol thick jungle filled with enemy soldiers every day. Another private at the same base, whose tent was just a few feet away, might work eight hours a day typing letters in an air-conditioned trailer.

Being in the Air Force or Navy was no guarantee of safety either. Airbases were targets of enemy rocket and mortar fire. One Air Force soldier, trained as a weather observer, was sent to a lonely—and dangerous—Army base deep in the Mekong Delta. Pilots needed the weather information he collected. Naval crews running gunboats up and down the Delta's rivers and canals always drew fire. Almost all U.S. soldiers came under mortar or rocket attack at one time or another. The shelling usually lasted only minutes, and there were bunkers made of sandbags for protection.

Soldiers in the "boondocks" (remote or hostile areas) knew that other servicemen lived well on large bases and in big cities. When on leave in Saigon they had seen these American soldiers and their Vietnamese girlfriends riding in jeeps and on motor scooters. This hurt morale. Morale is how a soldier feels about being in the military.

Differences between the lives of officers and enlisted men caused other morale problems. The military has always given officers more privileges and benefits, rewards for the difficult job of being in command and being responsible for others. Young soldiers didn't realize the burdens that came with the privileges. In their eyes, ordinary soldiers took the risks, and officers received the rewards.

There were other reasons for the growing resentment between officers and enlisted men. In Viet-

Two airborne soldiers wait anxiously for the enemy to appear.

nam, officers were required to be in combat for only six months of their twelve-month tour of duty. Enlisted men could be in combat all twelve months. This system prevented well-liked officers from staying with their men. As the war dragged on and the fighting grew more hazardous, new officers assigned to veteran troops lacked experience in jungle warfare and often made poor decisions. If their orders placed the soldiers in unnecessary danger, the troops at times disobeyed or even killed their own officers. An Army study showed that in one year, 209 officers were shot to death or blown up by their own troops. The real figure may have been higher. For these and other reasons, many young draftees refused to become officers.

The problems of noncommissioned officers were often overlooked as well. These officers were the sergeants and specialists who help make the armed forces work. Many were black, hispanic, or from other minority groups. They had spent their adult lives in the military, and many were married and had families. While serving in Vietnam could mean more money and faster promotions, it also put a strain on family relations and caused other problems for these soldiers. Trained in traditional warfare in such places as Germany, they were not prepared for the kind of combat they encountered in Vietnam. They often found themselves caught between young officers and even younger enlisted men.

Noncombat personnel were also at risk in this hot, humid combat zone. Doctors, nurses, chaplains, cooks, mechanics, and others worked within range of mortar and rocket attack. People outside the military also sustained alarming casualties. They included USAID (Agency for International Development) officials, missionaries, and reporters and photographers. Among the writers and photographers who died in Vietnam were Bernard Fall, a history professor whose books on Vietnam are considered among the best; François Sully, a correspondent for *Newsweek* magazine; and Sean Flynn, a photographer whose father was a movie star. Fall was killed by a land mine, Sully died in a helicopter crash, and Flynn dis-

Some photographers felt safer carrying M-16 rifles.

The enemy could be . . .

appeared after being taken prisoner near Cambodia.

Part of the reason everyone was at least in some danger was the fact that Vietnamese friend and foe looked exactly alike. Because the enemy could blend in so easily with the population, there was no such thing as established front lines where soldiers were separate from civilians. Any part of Vietnam could be a combat zone, and anyone from children to old people could be the enemy. Places safe one month could be thick with Viet Cong or NVA troops the next. While most areas were secure by day, nowhere was safe by night.

It is easy to see why many U.S. soldiers came to distrust and hate Vietnamese civilians. In a village where a booby trap wounded an American, the only people to blame were those in the village. The soldiers sometimes took out their frustration over the deaths or injuries of their friends on innocent Vietnamese people. However, considering the conditions under which these young soldiers fought, they often showed remarkable restraint and courage.

If the soldiers suffered, the civilian population suffered even more. A Vietnamese farmer often found himself in a situation with no good choices. For example, there could be large numbers of Viet Cong in his village. If he were unfriendly, they might harm him. If he acted friendly, another villager might tell Americans or South Vietnamese soldiers that he was a Viet Cong. If many people in his village sympathized with the enemy, then enemy soldiers were hidden when U.S. or South Vietnamese soldiers arrived. If the village was neutral, the Viet Cong could simply hide among the people. But a careless word by a child or an elderly person about the presence of VC could bring down destruction and death—from all sides. The American or South Vietnamese forces might burn the village, while VC or NVA fighters might kill people they regarded as informers.

Even swamps, forests, and places where there were few villages could be dangerous to civilians. Many of these areas became known as free-fire zones, areas where soldiers and pilots could fire at will. Civilians who

. . . a friend by day.

47

entered these suspected enemy areas did so at risk to their lives. B-52 bombers hit free-fire zones without warning. Jet fighters returning from a mission were allowed to drop leftover bombs in free-fire zones, and artillery pounded such areas around the clock. Bulldozers with huge, V-shaped plows ripped through the jungles looking for concealed enemy hideouts.

Although the enemy could strike anywhere at any time, there was more hope for wounded U.S. and ARVN soldiers in Vietnam than in any previous war. Helicopters could reach many wounded men who might have died without quick treatment. Ground forces could quickly clear a landing area with chain saws and explosives for rescue helicopters. In thick forests, wounded men were hoisted out of the thicket in slings dropped from a hovering aircraft. No longer did an injured man risk dying of shock or blood loss by being carried for hours on a stretcher. No one wanted to be wounded, but the odds of surviving a wound were very good.

At the height of the fighting, there were 16 U.S. Army hospitals, with 5 more under construction. Even though Vietnam was about 1,000 miles long, no soldier was more than 100 air miles from an operating room. The most common wounds were caused by shrapnel—the jagged, hot metal created when an artillery or mortar shell explodes. Rifle fire was the leading cause of death, largely because of the number of multiple wounds from automatic weapons. The rifles used were the Russian AK-47 and the American M-16. The bullets traveled at high speed and made large exit wounds as they left the body. Other causes of many injuries included VC booby traps and mines.

Because of the highly efficient medical treatment, four of every five wounded soldiers were able to return to duty. A wounded man was awarded a medal called the Purple Heart. Three Purple Hearts earned a combat soldier a job away from the fighting.

In contrast, North Vietnamese and Viet Cong soldiers were more likely to be wounded and less likely to survive their wounds. There were no modern hospitals to care for them in South Vietnam. They did have modern medicine, much

Fighting in some places meant war among the rice paddies.

of it obtained from black market sources in Saigon or Cambodia. But VC and NVA hospitals were either huts or tunnels with poor sanitation. In a single series of battles late in the war, the NVA suffered 100,000 casualties. That was twice the number suffered by the U.S. in all of 1968, the war's most brutal year. The rain gear carried by an NVA soldier all too often became a bag to haul his body into hiding.

Civilian casualties in North Vietnam began with the U.S. bombing in 1964 and did not end for almost ten years. As many as one million North Vietnamese soldiers and civilians died in Vietnam during the war. The bombing raids also created a great deal of hardship, destroying homes, public buildings, bridges, and more. Able-bodied North Vietnamese were put to work rebuilding ruined factories, roads, bridges, and dams. This prevented them from farming or otherwise earning a living. They had no luxuries and barely enough necessities.

On the other hand, America smothered South Vietnam in luxury items. PXs, the stores for soldiers, bulged with TV sets, radios, cameras, jewelry, clocks, tape recorders, candy, cigarettes, magazines, newspapers, soft drinks, and beer. Prices were cheap: a can of soda cost ten or fifteen cents. The PXs offered such services as barber shops, laundries, film processing, and custom tailoring. Tailors sewed patches on uniforms and made special-order suits. Even PX stores in outlying areas had at least a few luxury goods. Because these items were unloaded at major ports, the cigarettes, liquor, and food quickly turned up for sale on city streets. Items stolen in the morning found their way to the black market in the afternoon.

Another commodity sold throughout South Vietnam were illegal drugs. Marijuana became as common as chewing gum, and heroin could be purchased that carried brand names such as Tiger or Double Globe. Vietnamese in rural areas chewed betel nut, a mild relaxer that turned the teeth maroon, but few could afford illegal drugs. Some American soldiers, looking for ways to forget the war, sniffed or injected heroin and became addicted to the drug. Thousands smoked marijuana, which was less expensive and always available.

One soldier, who drove an armored personnel carrier, remembers how easy it was to get marijuana. "For two dollars, I bought a carton of cigarettes at the PX. I tossed the carton to an old Vietnamese guy. The next day, I gave him ten dollars and he gave me a carton of marijuana cigarettes. He had opened the carton and the packs, pulled the tobacco out of all 200 cigarettes, filled the cigarettes with marijuana and sealed it all back up. I carried a pack on me and it looked like I just had cigarettes." Marijuana was seldom smoked in the field or on guard duty, but it could be found on most military base camps. It was one more sign of unhappy soldiers in an unpopular war. "What could they do to me if they caught me with marijuana?" asked the personnel carrier driver. "Send me to Vietnam?"

Very little about Vietnam and the conflict made sense to many Americans. Perhaps because Vietnam was so remote, there was little popular enthusiasm for the war, and enlistments in the armed forces lagged. The Pentagon as

A U.S. Army officer examines confiscated drugs.

51

early as May 1965 talked about an all-volunteer army to fight the war. Such talk ended when military officials discovered that recruiting volunteers would cost the armed forces an extra $3 billion to $5 billion a year.

Officials decided to maintain the draft, a way of automatically bringing young men into the armed forces after they reached the age of 18. At about the same time, General Lewis B. Hershey, head of the draft, spoke out against deferments. These were delays in the draft granted to young men for a variety of reasons, such as ill health or continuing a college education. Hershey wanted to build up the military forces as much as possible to reinforce and replace troops already in Vietnam.

The military had good reason to be nervous about the draft. Not only was antiwar feeling growing in the United States, but stories about the fighting conditions in Vietnam were beginning to filter back home. Marines defending the airbase at Danang put up with eight-foot high elephant grass, heat stroke, wild boars, scorpions, leeches, all types of booby traps,

and even swarms of frogs, locusts, and mosquitoes. Vietnam was like nothing the Marines had ever seen before.

The flow of news did not work both ways, however. Radio, television, and a daily newspaper were available for American soldiers, but all of them were operated and censored by the U.S. government. Armed Forces Radio played rock, country, and black music and had brief, regularly scheduled newscasts, usually heavily censored. The television station showed programs from the U.S. and also had regular newscasts. The newspaper, *Stars and Stripes*, ran sports and general war news. But bad news, from Vietnam or from the U.S., was played down. The writers and editors of *Stars and Stripes* often fought the military over permission to report stories of large American losses or other bad news.

Soldiers found themselves in the middle of the world's biggest news story, yet they had little idea of what went on even a mile away. No one ever took a stroll just to look around. It was too dangerous. Ironically, the troops sometimes knew more about what was happening back home in the United States. For example, a tall, quiet member of the 9th Infantry Division named Calloway read a few lines in *Stars and Stripes* in 1967 about Detroit race riots. The article told of fires, gunfights, and killings and gave street names near Calloway's stateside home. How unusual that a young man facing enemy soldiers in Vietnam worried more about his family's safety than his own!

In Vietnam, however, the unusual was commonplace. For example, soldiers in many larger base camps had access to MARS stations. These were dozens of telephones linked to the United States by satellite. A soldier who didn't mind waiting for an available phone could call his parents or wife or girlfriend. The 12-hour time difference meant that his noon call would be received about midnight in the U.S. A soldier could talk to his parents in the morning; be in a firefight, or battle, that afternoon; then return to base and call his family again.

In addition to fighting the Viet Cong and NVA, Americans at times fought each other. Enlisted

General Lewis B. Hershey.

men's clubs at military bases were sometimes the scenes of barroom brawls. Soldiers, drunk on inexpensive beer, fought over such matters as jukebox songs. Blacks wanted to hear soul music. Whites wanted rock or country-western tunes.

However, the fighting wasn't always divided along color lines. For example, antiwar soldiers often had more trouble with rural or southern whites than they did with blacks or latinos. There was also fighting in the stockades. These were places where soldiers were put when they broke military law. Big stockades, such as the Long Binh Jail (called "Camp LBJ"), had places most guards feared to enter. Murderers, heroin addicts, and other desperate men were held in Camp LBJ before being sent back to prison in the U.S.

If prison awaited some soldiers, a wonderful five or six days of leave from the war awaited many others. The military provided its men with "R and R," or rest and relaxation leaves. Soldiers were not allowed to return to the continental U.S., but they could go to Hawaii to meet their families. Other popular spots included Thailand, Malaysia, Japan, the Philippines, Taiwan, Hong Kong, and Australia. Each soldier was permitted one R and R leave for every 12 months of duty (the Marines served 13 months). Shorter leaves of three days were usually spent at safe Vietnam beach resorts such as Vung Tau.

Because of air transport, U.S. troops had the unsettling experience of being whisked in and out of the Vietnam War. They could be vacationing on a Sydney, Australia, beach one day and be back on jungle patrol in Vietnam the next. It was one more bizarre aspect of what was turning out to be a very strange war.

Writing letters and receiving mail helped to maintain morale.

# Chapter 4

# Troubles in the South

After President Diem and his family were overthrown in 1963, a series of different rulers ran South Vietnam until the middle of 1965. At that point generals Nguyen Cao Ky and Nguyen Van Thieu seized power. Ky was a U.S.-trained jet pilot and a favorite of many American officials. They liked the way he always wanted to hunt the enemy, and the way he talked about winning the war. They overlooked the fact that he didn't care much for the rights of individual citizens in his country. His title was prime minister, while Thieu was president. Before Ky had been in power for a year, he had angered leaders of the country's most popular religion, Buddhism.

Earlier, in 1963, Buddhist leaders and their followers had protested the rule of Diem and his family, who were Catholic. Some monks had been willing to commit suicide by burning themselves to death on busy streets. The world watched in horror as television cameras recorded the deaths. Buddhist protests eventually led to the downfall of the Diem family.

In 1966, the protests shifted north to the old capital city of Hué. Ky took Vietnamese Marines to Hué to confront rebel ARVN soldiers who supported the Buddhists. U.S. troops had to separate the two factions. The threat of civil war appeared frighteningly real as Buddhists continued to stage strikes in Saigon. Eventually, Ky attacked Buddhist monasteries in Danang and Hué. He captured or killed leaders or forced them to flee, which weakened the protest. The prime minister showed that he was strong, but the Buddhist protestors proved that he was not popular.

President Thieu, a more reasonable man, was technically the head of the South Vietnamese

Nguyen Cao Ky, South Vietnamese war hero and politician.

government at this time. He usually sat quietly and watched Ky's dramatic actions. It soon became clear that Ky was losing whatever public support the government had had. After consulting with the Americans, Thieu and Ky promised the South Vietnamese that they would soon have a constitution to spell out the rights of citizens and would have nationwide elections. The Buddhist uprising had forced the Saigon government to make some reforms. Although the government frequently accused Buddhist activists of being VC sympathizers, only one Buddhist monk was ever in a high position in the Viet Cong. He was born of Cambodian parents in the Mekong Delta, joined the enemy in 1964 and died during an American air strike in 1966.

While the South Vietnamese got ready to vote, the Viet Cong prepared to disrupt the election. The VC saw themselves as poor farmers and those in the Vietnamese government as rich city dwellers. The government wanted to use rural Vietnamese in the struggle against the VC. There was only one problem with this

**Nguyen Cao Ky**

*Nguyen Cao Ky (born September 8, 1930), South Vietnamese military and political leader; prime minister of South Vietnam in the late 1960s*

*People considered Nguyen Cao Ky brave, devious, a showoff, a schemer, and an honest soldier. This complex man was all of these things. Born in North Vietnam, Ky fought for the French against Ho Chi Minh's communist liberation movement. Ky traveled south after Vietnam was divided in 1954 and joined the small South Vietnamese air force. He soon proved himself a skilled pilot. American advisers liked him immediately. While many South Vietnamese merely talked about fighting the enemy, Ky actually did so.*

*He flew secret agents into North Vietnam for the CIA, and single-handedly put down an attempt to overthrow one of South Vietnam's many unstable governments. Once he entered the political arena, he soon joined forces with General Nguyen Van Thieu, the armed forces chief in South Vietnam.*

strategy: the rural Vietnamese *were* the VC. By 1966, many pro-government leaders in rural areas had either been killed or run off by the enemy. Terror was one way to bring a mayor (and his village) to their side.

The Viet Cong learned, however, that terror tactics lost them followers as well, and they changed their ways. They offered villagers land, status, and a voice in future government. Saigon troops offered no change. Therefore, if the revolution won, the peasants won. If the government won, the peasants lost. The Viet Cong knew what the Americans never learned—the group that controls the village controls the nation.

This fact was true because the village had always been the heart of Vietnamese life. Even city-dwelling Vietnamese returned to their village homes for religious holidays and celebrations. They wanted to be buried where they were born. There was little loyalty to big cities such as Saigon or Hué. That is why rural Vietnamese accepted the Viet Cong idea that the country was being overrun by "Ky's rebel troops." It was only a short step from that point to actively supporting the VC. The VC established several clubs to help villagers make that step: Farmers' Liberation Association, Women's Liberation Association, Student Liberation Association, and so on. No matter what or where you were, there was a VC club where you and your friends could feel at home. Even religious clubs and special clubs for highland-dwelling Montagnards existed. All were aimed at the liberation of Vietnam.

At the heart of the Viet Cong organization were the *cadres*. A cadre was one or more people who served a village or a neighborhood

Thieu ran the country almost by himself.

North Vietnamese forces won major victories in northern South Vietnam during 1975. Thieu pulled troops from throughout the country back to Saigon in an effort to defend the capital. As ARVN troops moved toward the city, North Vietnamese forces took over the provinces they left behind.

Thieu resigned on April 12, 1975, only nine days before NVA troops entered Saigon. He fled Vietnam, taking millions of dollars in gold with him. He now lives in Great Britain.

## Nguyen Van Thieu

*Nguyen Van Thieu (born April 5, 1923), army general and president of South Vietnam, 1967-1975*

*Thieu was as unassuming as Nguyen Cao Ky was flashy. His mild manner proved a disadvantage in the war, however; the more chaotic conditions became in South Vietnam, the less able Thieu became to make wise decisions.*

*The son of a small landowner, Thieu joined the communists as a young man. Quickly disillusioned, he switched sides and fought for the French. After the division of Vietnam, Thieu went south and worked his way up in the South Vietnamese army. He had a hand in overthrowing several governments after the death of President Diem in 1963. Thieu became chief of state in 1965 in a military government, with Ky as prime minister. He was elected president in 1967 and re-elected in 1971.*

*Thieu had the support of presidents Johnson and Nixon, who overlooked his harsher, often vindictive side. When the Americans pulled out of Vietnam 1973,*

as a combination police officer, priest, teacher, and politician. He or she got people help when they needed it, told them that the government in Saigon was evil, showed them how to dig tunnels to escape air raids, asked them for rice for VC soldiers, and taught them how to build booby traps and weapons. A good cadre was not only a neighbor but a hero in the eyes of village children.

In the country, where rural people had no television sets, no radios, and no newspapers, village residents listened eagerly to the cadres' stories. The villagers usually worked until dark and then ate their evening meal. Afterward, the cadre invited neighbors to a central gathering place and taught them about the

South Vietnamese markets thrived throughout the war.

Village life involved long, hard hours of work each day.

Viet Cong. This was done by telling heroic tales not by reading books. The men, women, and children who had worked all day in the dirt and heat relaxed and listened to the stories. Everything the Vietnamese valued was said of the Viet Cong: they respected their parents, they defended their village, they worshipped their ancestors. In contrast, news of government or American troops abusing villagers was repeated night after night. Atrocities, such as the actual eating by ARVN troops of a captured VC soldier's liver, were told all across the country. The cadres never mentioned abuses committed by the VC or North Vietnamese. No wonder rural people supported the enemy!

Once the Viet Cong declared an area "liberated," they began to set up their own government. If a South Vietnamese tax collector walked into this area, he or she was chased away or even killed. Large landowners were forced to give much of their farms to landless peasants. Schools were devoted to teaching everything from laying booby traps to planting trees. Weapons given by the U.S. and Saigon to villagers found their way into guerrilla hands. The VC in turn donated large first-aid kits to "liberated" villagers.

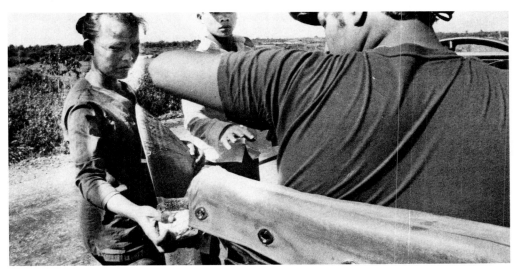
An American GI makes a drug buy on a lonely road.

Although the U.S. and South Vietnamese government could give villagers food, tools, weapons for defense, bags of cement, or wood and wire for construction, they had nothing to compare with the VC cadres. Throughout the war years, the Americans and South Vietnamese developed several plans to "win the hearts and minds" of the people. They even attempted to win over Viet Cong guerrillas. A plan called *chieu hoi*, Vietnamese for "open arms," promised the VC money, land, and a new life if they would come over to the South Vietnamese side. Those who accepted were called *hoi chanh*. Because dis-

trust of the Saigon government was so high, few VC surrendered. Without a group like the cadre, who were willing to live and work among the people, the South Vietnamese government never gained the people's support.

Some of the problems in the South came as the result of a clash between American and Vietnamese cultures. American officials found themselves baffled by the beliefs and characteristics of their South Vietnamese allies. The Vietnamese appeared to be very superstitious and to conduct many of their affairs according to mysterious signs and portents. When the Saigon government was creating the new constitution, for example, members looked to traditional lucky numbers, particularly the number 117, to help them shape the document. Exactly 117 deputies in the government worked on the new laws. The constitution was composed of 117 articles. The new laws were made public in April 1, 1967, a day suggested by astrologers as being very lucky. The date, April Fool's Day, had quite another meaning for the Americans.

Lucky day or not, the constitution did not fare well. Most rural Vietnamese never knew of its existence and, if given a copy, would have been unable to read it. Eventually, the document was forgotten by government officials.

If South Vietnamese superstitions puzzled Americans, the level of official corruption angered them. Even the Vietnamese, when speaking frankly, admitted there was considerable corruption in the Saigon government. For instance, officials illegally charged peasants money to provide them with identification papers, which everyone was required to carry. Without these papers, even a child could be arrested as a suspected Viet Cong. Officials accused of taking money from the peasants were simply shifted to other jobs rather than punished. This situation angered many American officials and private aid groups who worked with the poorer people in Vietnam.

Unfortunately, the United States was also partly to blame for the problems in South Vietnam. By bringing so much money and so many goods into the country, the Americans drove up prices. They created opportunities for wealth—both legal and illegal—where none had existed before. Many normally honest Vietnamese officials scrambled madly for their share of the money. Americans tried to help the situation by paying Vietnamese workers higher wages. A worker who filled sandbags at a U.S. Army division headquarters was paid 100 piastres (65 cents) for eight hours of labor, more than he or she could earn in many other jobs. Women set up shacks near base camps and sold soft drinks and beer for a dollar or more. In fact, children could support entire families by shining boots, washing jeeps, or doing other chores.

The black market featured stolen U.S. goods.

Robert McNamara, Secretary of Defense.

Despite the measures Americans took to control prices, they climbed higher and higher. The condition, known as inflation, created great economic hardships for many families. It made the American presence in Vietnam a source of continued resentment among the people.

Even those Vietnamese who had no direct contact with Americans often suffered economically.

The U.S. used thousands of gallons of defoliants (chemicals used to kill jungle plants), sprayed from low-flying planes. While such chemicals, like Agent Orange, killed off the jungle and denied the enemy places to hide, they also destroyed rice crops, fruit trees, and grazing lands. Farmers weren't always told that they could apply to the U.S. miliary to get payment for their ruined crops. Even if they managed to fill out all the proper forms, a corrupt Saigon official usually ended up with the money.

One man who was beginning to see the situation clearly in South Vietnam was the Secretary of Defense, Robert McNamara. He had taken on the secretarial position under President Kennedy. McNamara, who had been president of the Ford Motor company, was a brilliant organizer and helped plan the initial buildup in Vietnam. When President Johnson urged him to stay on as Secretary of Defense, McNamara agreed. He felt he still had work to do to make the armed forces more efficient.

It was during the Johnson years that McNamara's opinions on Vietnam began to change. As early as 1966, McNamara made several trips to Southeast Asia and noticed how badly things were going. He told reporters that everything was fine, but he informed President Johnson otherwise. He urged Johnson to find some way to negotiate a political solution to the war.

LBJ did not want to listen to what his Secretary of Defense had to say. A political settlement meant accepting either a communist government in the North or a communist faction in the government of a united Vietnam. Such an idea violated the United States' commitment to fight the spread of communism.

President Johnson turned more and more to hardline military men such as the Joint Chiefs of Staff, who headed the armed forces. This group believed we could win a military victory in Vietnam and supported even greater U.S. involvement in the war.

By the end of 1967, Johnson and his cabinet advisers made another fateful decision. From now on, American troops would bear the brunt of fighting the enemy while South Vietnamese troops would be given the job of guarding bases or securing an area after a battle had been fought. Military advisers, including General Westmoreland, believed this change in strategy would lead to victory. To fulfill this commitment, President Johnson authorized sending more troops to Southeast Asia. By December 1967, the original force of a few thousand soldiers had swollen to a

Nguyen Van Thieu reviews South Vietnamese troops.

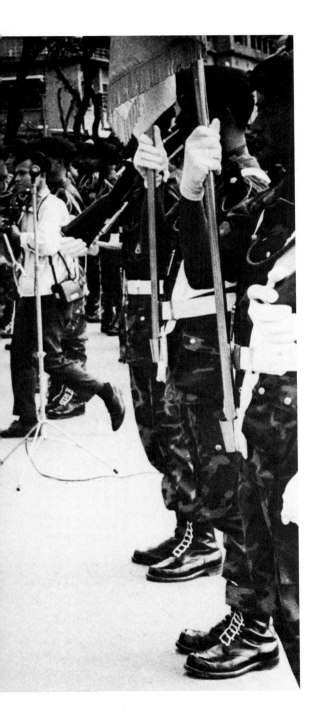

massive army of 500,000 troops.

However, the more involved Americans became in Vietnam, the more they failed to understand or become friends with the South Vietnamese. Villagers watched in amazement as helicopters were used to deliver hot meals to many infantry units on an operation. They wondered if the Americans were serious about helping them with problems of medical care, food shortages, and government corruption when time and money were expended to bring soldiers soft drinks, magazines, candy bars, and beer in the field. Many Vietnamese people resented the fact that Americans brought in hundreds of thousands of soldiers, then hired Vietnamese to do the worst jobs, like cleaning toilets or hauling garbage.

Many U.S. advisers and military personnel found they had come half way around the world to help save a country they neither liked nor understood. Although U.S. and South Vietnamese forces were winning on the battlefield, they were steadily losing the war for the hearts and minds of the Vietnamese people.

# Chapter 5

# Air War over Vietnam

The North Vietnamese survived eight years of almost constant bombing. What is more remarkable, they did so against the most modern aircraft and the best-trained pilots in the world. During those eight years, a million tons of bombs, more than had been dropped on Europe in all of World War II, rained down on a country no bigger than the state of Missouri.

Different kinds of bombs were designed for different targets. They were delivered by aircraft built especially for various missions, whether it was blowing up a bridge or destroying a line of trucks. Looking back, the U.S. air raids on North Vietnam proved both the strong and weak points of using aircraft in a modern war.

President Lyndon Johnson started the bombing in 1964 for several reasons. The enemy had attacked U.S. bases in South Vietnam, killing American soldiers.

They also chased U.S. warships in the South China Sea. The President decided to bomb the North to punish them for supporting the Viet Cong in the South and for waging war against South Vietnam. Once the bombing started, it escalated, or increased. Each time U.S. planes hammered the North, the Viet Cong retaliated by attacking Americans or by setting off powerful bombs on bases and in the cities that killed or injured soldiers and civilians. By 1965, the bombing of North Vietnam was constant. It was given a name, "Operation Rolling Thunder."

Anyone who has ever been on the ground in a bombing raid will tell you that rolling thunder is a good description. Even though people can hide in protected areas, there is little they can do as they hear and feel the bombs move toward them. The explosions hit faster than heartbeats and shake the ground violently.

Bombs fall from a U.S. fighter-bomber.

After a raid, people wander around with terrible headaches. They cannot focus their eyes, and they may be temporarily or permanently deafened from the blasts. They often bleed from the nose, mouth, or ears.

A person can be in a sheltered place and still be hurt badly by the bombs' shock waves, or concussions. Some bombs create a powerful concussion. Others, such as phosphorus or napalm, generate heat fierce enough to melt metal. Napalm sticks to the skin as it burns, causing horrible, painful injuries. Cluster bombs open in midair, spilling hundreds of smaller bombs over a wide area. Other kinds of explosives with delayed fuses were also used. Landing harmlessly on the ground, these bombs blow up hours or even days after an air raid.

President Johnson and his advisers wanted the bombing to break the will of the North Vietnamese. Instead, it did just the opposite. People came together determined to fight and survive. Those too old or too young to join the army eagerly learned how to fire antiaircraft guns and how to

Napalm dropped near a South Vietnamese outpost.

shoot SAM (surface-to-air) missiles at attacking planes. The country became completely mobilized to fight a long battle.

In addition to guns and missiles on the ground, the North had MiG jet fighters. These Russian-made jets, first seen during the Korean War, were slower and lighter than most U.S. aircraft. The enemy pilots, although well trained, were outnumbered. For every U.S. plane shot down by a MiG, about seven MiGs were lost. Dogfights—aerial combat between jets—took place through-out 1966. Early in 1967, the North Vietnamese lost seven planes in a single day. Later in the year, President Johnson permitted U.S. aircraft to attack MiG bases. Those attacks, combined with 137 total MiG losses in dogfights, made enemy aircraft less of a hazard than ground fire.

The U.S. was also constantly losing planes and pilots. Yet whenever a multimillion-dollar craft was shot down, it could be quickly replaced. These airplanes were truly modern wonders. They could travel at speeds in excess of 1,000 miles an hour and had after-burners that gave them sudden

A U.S. Air Force F-105 scores a direct hit on a North Vietnamese MiG.

73

boosts of power to outrun the enemy. Their electronic equipment was a marvel. The pilots who flew them had hundreds of hours of training and were older and more experienced than were American ground forces.

The pilots often played deadly electronic warfare with the North Vietnamese. The enemy had thousands of SAM missiles pointed at the skies. Whenever their radar "locked" on a U.S. plane, the missiles were fired. Once in the air, they were kept on course by a radio transmitter. A missile chased the aircraft until it either hit the plane or lost it and ran out of fuel. At first, American pilots flew in low over the targets so SAM radar had no time to lock onto their planes. In response, the enemy increased its antiaircraft fire, which hit many low-flying U.S. planes.

Returning to higher altitudes to escape ground fire, the Americans used a radar-jamming trick first tried in World War II. They dropped thousands of small bits of aluminum foil to fool the SAM radar. They also used a new missile that turned the tables on the surface-to-air missiles. Flying

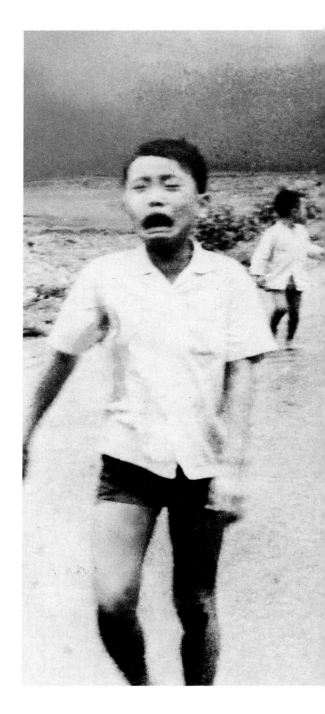

Burned children run from napalm accidentally dropped where they hid.

Ground maintenance on an F-4 Phantom jet.

into North Vietnam, a U.S. plane picked up SAM radar beams with special electronic gear that pinpointed its base. The pilot fired a small missile that "rode" the radar beam back down to the SAM base, blowing up the missile and its radar. The enemy, in turn, began to play tricks with its radar that sometimes fooled the pilot armed with the anti-SAM missiles.

A skilled pilot had a good chance of dodging a SAM. Once his plane was targeted by SAM radar, warning lights went off in his cockpit. The pilot knew the missile was aiming for him. At times he could see it clearly on a sunny day. One pilot recalled that some of the later SAMs were "the size of telephone poles." As the missile neared, the pilot made a sudden, sharp turn or roll with his plane. The SAM went past him and could not turn around. SAMs were often fired in groups, however, so that if a pilot dodged one missile he would be hit by a SAM fired a few seconds later.

Although in times of danger a pilot could feel very alone in the sky, many other planes and pilots were in the air to assist him. Some flew special planes equipped with radar and jamming devices. These unarmed planes could warn jets on bombing runs of missiles and of enemy planes heading toward them. Huge tankers could be called in to refuel aircraft in the air. Refueling often took place before and after a raid, because planes carried little fuel in order to pack in more bombs. Several rescue planes and helicopters also waited off North Vietnamese shores. These craft could move in quickly to look for—and possibly rescue—pilots who were shot down. Even today, the list of more than 2,400 men missing in action from the war shows that many pilots were lost over South Vietnam and Laos.

Helicopters turned out to be the backbone of aerial operations in South Vietnam. The most common helicopter was the Bell UH or Huey. Capable of carrying up to 14 men (or serving as an ambulance, a gunship, or a command craft), the turbine-powered helicopter was the first vehicle to set down in a combat landing zone. Large troop carriers, such as the buslike Chinooks, were able to carry artillery in slings beneath

U.S. Army cavalry troops return from Cambodia.

them. Other commonly used helipcopters were the cargo-hauling Tarhe Sky Crane and the Bell Kiowa observation chopper. Tiny, unarmed, two-man observation or "bubble" helicopters were used to spot enemy positions and to call in artillery or air strikes.

Two propeller-driven planes also played major roles in South Vietnam. One was the C-47, a cargo plane used in World War II. It was equipped with machine guns fired out of the plane's side door and windows. The plane was soon nicknamed "Puff the Magic Dragon" or "Spooky" by the troops because it could pour out 6,000 red tracer bullets a minute. At that rate, in 60 seconds it could riddle every square foot of an area the size of a football field. The amount of firepower it delivered was simply unbelievable. Seen at night, the bullets looked like a waterfall of red fire pouring down on an enemy position.

The other propeller plane was the A-1 Skyraider, a fighter-bomber that carried large quantities of bombs, rockets, and cannon shells. It flew much slower than a jet and for that reason was very accurate in hitting enemy ground positions. It could stay in the air for a long time and could move back and forth over a target without taking miles to turn around. Its engines thumped rhythmically, unlike the high-pitched scream of the jets. A 9th Infantry Division soldier remembers the difference between a jet and a Skyraider. "The first time I heard a Skyraider, I thought it was a Chevrolet."

Two more modern planes were enlisted in the air war—the F-4 Phantom and the B-52 Stratofortress bomber. The Phantom was used by Air Force, Marine, and Navy flyers for raids over North and South Vietnam and later over Cambodia and Laos. The plane had one pilot and a second flyer who sat directly behind him to run the radar. Fast, heavy, and large, these planes could be seen over the Ho Chi Minh Trail, streaking across the Delta, or diving toward a North Vietnamese bridge. They were often radar-directed, which meant that bad weather could not prevent them from finding their targets.

In contrast to the Phantoms, which attacked high or low, B-52 Stratofortress bombers flew miles

Propeller-driven Skyraider planes were used in combat.

above a target. They hit carefully selected areas, sometimes as close as one-quarter mile from friendly forces. B-52s were occasionally shot down by SAM missiles over Vietnam, which meant that a crew of six had to survive a crash and then probable capture. These awkward but reliable bombers at first flew out of Pacific island bases. As the war continued and the bombing escalated, most B-52s were moved to Thailand, only a few hours from any possible target. Designed originally to carry nuclear weapons, these planes dropped non-nuclear bombs on South Vietnam, Laos, and Cambodia for nearly eight years.

Vietnam was truly an air war in many ways. Soldiers just arriving in the country were flown to assignments in transport planes, which were used everywhere. The 173rd Airborne Division jumped from these aircraft in 1967 during Operation Junction City. Soldiers going to or returning from R and R leave used transport planes as if they were commercial shuttle buses. Marines, surrounded in Khe Sanh in the highlands by thousands of North Vietnamese Army soldiers, got supplies and ammunition from the planes. While these slow, propeller-driven aircraft were not fancy, they could shrug off ground fire and land safely on rough airfields.

Anyone seeing how many aircraft and bombs the Americans brought with them had good reason to think the war would be over soon. Yet the North Vietnamese continued to fight. To Secretary of Defense Robert McNamara, the failure of the bombing raids was an ominous sign for the U.S. and its allies.

An American fighter-bomber takes off from a carrier in the South China Sea.

# Chapter 6

# Bringing the War Home

A soldier or government official returning from Vietnam to the United States in 1967 might not have recognized the country. Young people wore strange tunic-like shirts, bell-bottom pants, beads, flowers in their hair, and peace symbols. Even the boys let their hair grow long and sported mustaches and beards.

The young people talked openly about drug use, sex, and dropping out of school. They listened to rock groups with names like the Beatles, Led Zeppelin, Lovin' Spoonful, Rolling Stones, Jefferson Airplane, and the Grateful Dead. Folk musicians Joan Baez and Bob Dylan sang about the changes sweeping the land.

In California, a free-speech movement started at the University of California in Berkeley. It set off a chain reaction of student protests that eventually spread to campuses across the country. In some schools, such as Columbia University, students even took over administration buildings, insisting that the University president and his staff meet with them to discuss their demands. Students for a Democratic Society (SDS), founded in the early 1960s, often took the lead in campus demonstrations.

The hippie movement, with its emphasis on peace and love, started about the same time in San Francisco and caught on across the country. Many hippies emphasized drug use and open sex. They advocated a return to more "natural" ways, including living off the land and using only natural materials in clothing, housing, and toolmaking. They believed large corporations and government bureaucracies exploited people and natural resources purely for their own profit.

The hippies called for a different system based on barter and the free exchange of goods and services. Many lived together in communes and tried to estab-

Younger Americans formed the backbone of the antiwar protests.

lish a more ideal way of life. War was incompatible with this ideal. But some of their actions and their heavy drug use, including the hallucinatory drug LSD, ultimately hurt the antiwar cause. They angered the more conservative people whom the protest movement wanted to reach.

The young people's appearance wasn't the only thing that made them radically different from their parents. Many of them were also beginning to oppose the war in Southeast Asia. Night after night they saw images of the war on television — villages being bombed, one government after another falling in Saigon, children burned with napalm running from the battlefield, U.S. troops fighting an enemy that seemed to vanish and reappear like mist. They heard Johnson talk about preserving democracy in South Vietnam, but the Saigon government appeared little better than the communists. They began to ask why the U.S. was involved in Vietnam at all.

Most conservative and older Americans silently backed the Johnson administration's war policies. But the teenagers and young adults, many of them faced with the prospect of being sent to Vietnam, decided to act on their beliefs and doubts about the war. They had watched civil rights demonstrators on television and had learned how to run a successful protest. Sparked by a small group of serious antiwar leaders, the movement grew quickly.

Beginning in 1965, antiwar "teach-ins" were held on several campuses. These teach-ins continued over several days and were designed to inform people about the history of Southeast Asia and the origins of the current conflict. They tried to show the public why the U.S. policies were misguided and why the government should get out of Vietnam. Ironically, because of the war, thousands of people were now learning about this distant country.

Opposing the antiwar demonstrators were those who supported the war effort. A majority of college and university students, the American Legion, Veterans of Foreign Wars, and other civic and patriotic groups believed the conflict in Vietnam was necessary to contain communism. If we did not stop communists in Saigon, they

Demonstrators were seen most often in Washington, D.C.

reasoned, then we could end up fighting them in Hawaii or even in San Francisco. The debate between antiwar and prowar factions gradually took a violent turn.

Those returning from Vietnam saw scenes at home that were eerie reminders of the war they had left behind. Urban riots set off fires that lit up the skies in Detroit, Chicago, New York, and Los Angeles—and looked just like firefights in Southeast Asia. There were troops patroling the streets to keep order. There were demonstrations every bit as well

Burning Selective Service or draft cards.

organized as the Buddhist protests in Vietnam. Even more disturbing, a few antiwar extremists imitated some of the Buddhist monks by burning themselves to death to protest the war. With Vietnam assuming more importance than civil rights or the economy, a veteran might feel that he hadn't left the war behind at all.

One strong symbol of protest throughout this period was the burning of draft cards. Federal law stated that young men had to register for the military draft when they reached 18 years of age. They signed up at Selective Service offices in every state county and received a wallet card that proved they had registered. Registration created a list of men who could be drafted, or taken into military service. It was illegal to avoid registering, and it was illegal to destroy a draft card once you had registered.

To show their opposition to the war, hundreds of students and others gathered at demonstrations and set their cards afire. Very few ended up in prison. While white, middle-class young adults protested, the country drafted many blacks, hispanics, and poor or blue-collar whites to fight overseas. The division of draftees along economic lines continued throughout the war.

By 1966, as many as 50,000 young men a month were getting notices from the government to take physical exams for military service. Many of those who had no deferment (a reason for not being drafted) tried to avoid the draft in a number of ways. They tried to flunk their physical exam. They escaped to Canada. They became conscientious objectors, that is, persons whose beliefs do not allow them to take part in war. They claimed to be drug addicts. A musician from eastern Ohio even told the local draft board secretary that he would kill her if she tried to induct him. "I wasn't really going to kill her, but it scared her so badly she must have thrown my file away." On the other hand, many men who feared front-line action actually joined the military. They chose three- to six-year enlistments in safe jobs rather than a two-year draft that could mean being sent to Vietnam.

As early as mid-1966 a few Selective Service offices around

the country began to run low on the number of eligible men to draft. They called up married men with no more than one child and others who ordinarily would not be regarded as fit for military service. A basic training company at Fort Knox, Kentucky, in September 1966, for example, contained a man who had managed to volunteer for the Army while in prison in Michigan; a married man with only one lung; and several men with legal, physical, or personal problems. The convict ran away, but most of the others made it through eight weeks of training.

President Johnson, his advisers, and the military men in the U.S. and Vietnam bitterly resented the antiwar movement. They waged a determined public relations campaign to gain support for the war. They talked about the gains in South Vietnam, the economic aid to rural areas, the buildup of the South Vietnamese army, and the number of enemy troops killed, wounded, and captured. McNamara, with his emphasis on facts and figures, began to appear somewhat cold and computer-like to a public who was viewing the hardships of war on television.

Ironically, the administration's press conferences ended up aiding the antiwar movement. In order to gain support, Johnson and his advisers sometimes lied to the American people about how the war was going. On more than one occasion, they were caught in these lies by alert reporters or by people within the administration who were increasingly unhappy with the war. These government employees leaked information to the press that showed the administration and military leaders were painting too rosy a picture of the situation in Vietnam. This picture did not match what people were learning about the war: continued enemy gains, greater numbers of U.S. pilots in North Vietnamese prisoner-of-war camps, and the steady stream of aluminum coffins from Vietnam arriving every day at a warehouse in Oakland, California.

As the war escalated, the protest movement changed from being a fringe activity supported mainly by radical students and hippies to a more middle-class movement. Parents and children who once had been deeply divided

President Johnson (right) and his advisers did not know how to react to war protestors.

## J. William Fulbright

*J. William Fulbright (born April 9, 1905), U.S. senator from Arkansas 1945-1975; chairman of the Senate Foreign Relations Committee*

*Senator Fulbright was one of the influential members of Congress who helped President Lyndon B. Johnson pass the Tonkin Gulf Resolution in 1964. The Resolution was the first major step in widening the war in Vietnam. Fulbright quickly came to regret the part he played as he learned more about the conflict.*

*The act allowed the President to attack North Vietnam without consulting Congress and gave many other powers to the President that were usually reserved to Congress. As early as 1965, Fulbright told the Presdient privately that a ground war in Asia would end in disaster for the United States.*

*Fulbright, in an important speech to fellow senators, called for negotiations with the North Vietnamese. He conducted hearings on the war that embarrassed Johnson and his advisers.*

*Although two other senators, Wayne Morse of Oregon and Ernest Gruening of Alaska, opposed the war even earlier than Fulbright, no one became a more respected voice for peace in Vietnam.*

over the war were now marching side by side in the same demonstrations. With each protest, more middle-class Americans took part. They found government policies confusing, and they began to doubt that the administration really knew how to win in Vietnam.

While the war was being opposed in the streets, an increasing number of Congressmen voiced their opposition as well. Those who opposed the war and urged the administration to find a diplomatic solution to the conflict became known as "doves," named after the symbolic bird of peace. Those who supported a military solution and continued to vote for escalating the war were called "hawks," after the bird of prey. In time, anyone who opposed or supported the war was labeled a dove or a hawk. Even Johnson's own cabinet eventually became a tug-of-war between hawks and doves.

No politician on Capitol Hill opposed the war more effectively than did Arkansas Senator J. William Fulbright, who had once been a hawk. In 1964, the Senator had helped President Johnson

President Johnson tried to deflect attention from antiwar hearings by meeting Nguyen Cao Ky in Hawaii.

commit troops to Vietnam by supporting the Tonkin Gulf Resolution, but he quickly regretted his action. As chairman of the Senate Foreign Relations Committee, he conducted hearings in January and February 1966 on America's involvement in Southeast Asia. A brilliant man who was not afraid of a powerful President, Fulbright and his committee pressed Secretary of State Dean Rusk, General Maxwell Taylor, Robert McNamara, and others to tell the country why we should continue the war in Vietnam.

LBJ attempted to steal headlines by meeting with South Vietnam Prime Minister Ky in Hawaii. Ky told the press that U.S. and South Vietnamese troops were pushing the enemy back toward the North and searching out enemy strongholds in the South. Soon they would be able to negotiate a peace settlement with North Vietnam.

Fulbright's hearings, however, showed that antiwar feelings in the United States were growing, and not just among the public. Two kinds of senators now opposed the war—those who were against it on moral grounds and those who felt LBJ had failed to consult them about escalating the fighting. The moral questions were becoming the most troublesome. If, in order to win the war, U.S. forces had to bomb civilians and devastate their land, what kind of victory would we attain? Would the people be better off under a South Vietnamese government that cared little for their rights?

The hearings continued for several weeks. When they ended, Senator Fulbright and LBJ, who had once been friends, never spoke to each other again.

The war was also costing the United States some of its friends abroad. In 1965, Charles de Gaulle, the French World War II hero and president of France, began criticizing the U.S. about its involvement in Vietnam. When the U.S. ignored his warnings, de Gaulle withdrew from NATO, the anticommunist defense organization in Europe. Young people in Germany, Great Britain, and Scandinavia also staged anti-American protests and called for the U.S. to leave Vietnam. Canadians took in Americans who sought to avoid the draft or who

Charles DeGaulle.

were deserters either from the war or from American military bases.

Other nations supported the U.S. involvement in Vietnam and offered their help. Australia, New Zealand, South Korea, Thailand, and the Philippines all sent troops to fight the enemy in Vietnam. The Korean, Thai, and Filipino governments were paid by the U.S. for these services, because equipping a military force was costly for these nations.

As the war dragged on, administration officials even turned to some communist states that might be willing to talk to North Vietnam about peace. Averell Harriman, a roving ambassador for the U.S., spoke with several communist and neutral representatives about the possibility of peace talks. The government in Hanoi knew that Americans would be serious about peace only if they grew tired of the war. In the late 1960s, they did not seem tired, bombing North Vietnam whenever weather permitted. The government in Hanoi hinted they were ready to talk but only about a political solution. They would not accept the government of South Vietnam. As the political sparring went on, casualties mounted on both sides.

Meanwhile, young Americans were dodging the draft in earnest. The most famous protestor was Muhammad Ali, world heavyweight boxing champion. He had become a Muslim during his boxing career and said that his religion prohibited him from participating in the war. Ali was tried and convicted of draft evasion, fined $10,000, and sentenced to a five-year jail term. He appealed the verdict and, years later, the conviction was overturned.

## W. Averell Harriman

*W. Averell Harriman (1891-1986), U.S. diplomat in the Vietnam era under presidents Kennedy, Johnson, and Nixon*

*Averell Harriman represented the United States in meetings with other countries for 28 years. The son of a wealthy railroad owner, Harriman served as a governor, an ambassador, and as Secretary of Commerce under President Truman. A skilled diplomat, he believed in dealing fairly with the Soviet Union and even negotiated a nuclear test-ban treaty with the Russians.*

*His most important role in the Vietnam conflict was serving as President Johnson's ambassador to the Paris peace talks with North Vietnam in 1968 and 1969. He even approached the Soviet Union during the Johnson administration to see if they could talk the North Vietnamese into a truce. In the Kennedy administration, Harriman had been known for his firm stance with South Vietnam's often weak leaders. A strong realist, he told antiwar activists in 1970 that President Nixon would be wise to listen to them.*

Muhammad Ali (left) was prosecuted for his refusal to join the war effort.

Despite Ali's victory in court, the commissioners who ran the sport of boxing took away his heavyweight crown. They may have been pressured by the government to do so.

If the government could put pressure on people, why couldn't the people put pressure on the government? College students in the fall of 1967 began to step up their protest activities. They picketed and boycotted military recruiters who came on campus looking for seniors to recruit as future officers. Companies that made weapons and explosives, such as Dow Chemical, and government agencies like the CIA tried without success to attract future employees. Students would surround recruiting offices, preventing anyone from getting near them. At times the demonstrations were broken up by police with tear gas and nightsticks. Students tried to follow the guidelines of nonviolence, but more than once confrontations with the police erupted in fighting. Many police were not trained to handle crowds or demonstrators, and some protestors focused on taunting any representatives of authority.

One of the largest protest marches took place in October 1967 as nearly 50,000 people marched on the Pentagon, the U.S. military headquarters in Washington, D.C. Organized by veterans of antiwar demonstrations from both coasts, the march resulted in many arrests after protestors tried to enter Pentagon grounds. Among those deeply committed to pacifism, or the peaceful resolution of conflict, was the famed baby doctor, Dr. Benjamin Spock. The older people arrested in the demonstration were treated well by government forces and the police, but numerous students were badly beaten. This march clearly showed that antiwar protestors were serious about wanting to end the war and that the government was equally determined to prevent them from interfering. As both sides became more convinced they were right, they turned to more violent behavior.

One band of men and women with direct experience in the war were also beginning to have a growing impact on the public. This group, Vietnam Veterans Against the War (VVAW), was founded in the spring of 1967. A few veterans who had met at a New York City antiwar rally decided that their views should be heard as well. Who better could speak against the war than those who had fought in it? Although their membership was never large, many veterans who were otherwise proud of their conduct in Vietnam supported VVAW-

Clergymen lead marchers toward the Pentagon in 1967.

backed projects to focus public attention on the effects of the war.

These projects included trying to get help for veterans who suffered health problems as the result of handling chemical defoliants such as Agent Orange. The organization also led the way in getting better veterans' benefits and in helping former soldiers get treatment for their mental and emotional problems caused by experiences in the war. The 7,000 members of VVAW showed the American public a side of the combat soldier seldom seen by civilians.

Americans against the war tried to keep the issues alive on the front page. They took to the streets, made the public aware of U.S. war policies, helped wounded or otherwise troubled veterans, passed out handbills, endured arrest, and nursed wounds from nightsticks and boots. Their aim was to bring the agony of war home to the American people and to bring American soldiers home from the war.

# Chapter 7

# Trouble Ahead

Can a fence stop an army? Usually not. But as the number of U.S. casualties rose during 1967, Secretary of Defense Robert McNamara began to think a lot about fences. He wanted to build one along the demilitarized zone that separated North and South Vietnam. A fence that ran across Vietnam and into Laos would cut the Ho Chi Minh Trail. Despite repeated bombings along the trail, more and more NVA troops and supplies were coming south.

There weren't enough Americans or South Vietnamese to make a human fence. Instead, McNamara wanted a space-age fence that could smell, hear, and see enemy soldiers as they crossed the DMZ. A barrier like that could tell U.S. experts where and when enemy soldiers should be stopped.

McNamara talked the idea over with President Johnson and his military advisers. They agreed it was worth a try, and the Pen-

tagon's weapons experts went to work. By the fall of 1967, most of the hardware devices for McNamara's space-age fence were ready to be placed in and around the DMZ.

Many of the devices were dropped from aircraft. As they landed, they sprouted antennas and lay in wait for enemy soldiers. Noises, vibrations, or scents triggered sensitive electronic receivers in the devices, which sent coded signals to a nearby military base. The base commanders decided what action to take.

An electronic, space-age fence sounded good on paper, but it failed in the field. The idea was symbolic of the many tactics that went wrong in Vietnam. Enemy soldiers destroyed a sensor whenever they found one. Wild animals often set the sensors off, triggering false alarms at a military base. Even the sensors that detected odors didn't work very

A paratrooper looks for the enemy in northern South Vietnam.

well in the hot, humid air.

These and other exotic ideas showed that McNamara and his staff were looking for any method to turn the situation around in Vietnam. The Secretary of Defense was in the unhappy position of having to report to Congress that there was little progress in the war. A glance at the statistics told the story. America was spending three dollars to destroy one dollar's worth of enemy materiél in North Vietnam. It made little sense to bomb targets that were of small value to the enemy.

Other figures involved the cost of fighting an enemy whose troop strength seemed inexhaustible. According to reports by U.S. and Vietnamese field commanders, the NVA had suffered so many casualties they should have been out of troops. But enemy soldiers who died were replaced almost overnight. According to military records, it cost the U.S. more than $8,000 for every enemy soldier killed. As someone suggested dryly, why not just pay the enemy not to fight?

To make matters worse, the South Vietnamese ARVN soldiers were not doing well. After American forces cleared an area, the South Vietnamese were supposed to move in and work with the people, winning their hearts and minds for the Saigon government. ARVN commanders felt this role was beneath them. Thus, the very people who knew the language and customs of rural Vietnam best had little contact with its people.

The American public did not know that in northern South Vietnam the enemy had so much influence there was not a single village American intelligence considered "friendly." U.S. forces in the area, including the 1st and 3rd Marine divisions and the Army's 1st Cavalry, 4th, and Americal divisions, hardly saw any "friendlies" during their stay.

Having control of the countryside around the DMZ gave the NVA army an enormous advantage. They increased their military operations in 1967 in the area just below the demilitarized zone. The Marines responded by bringing more troops into the field. The two sides finally clashed in one of the bloodiest battles of the war near the valley of Khe Sanh.

Khe Sanh guarded the friendly side of the demilitarized zone.

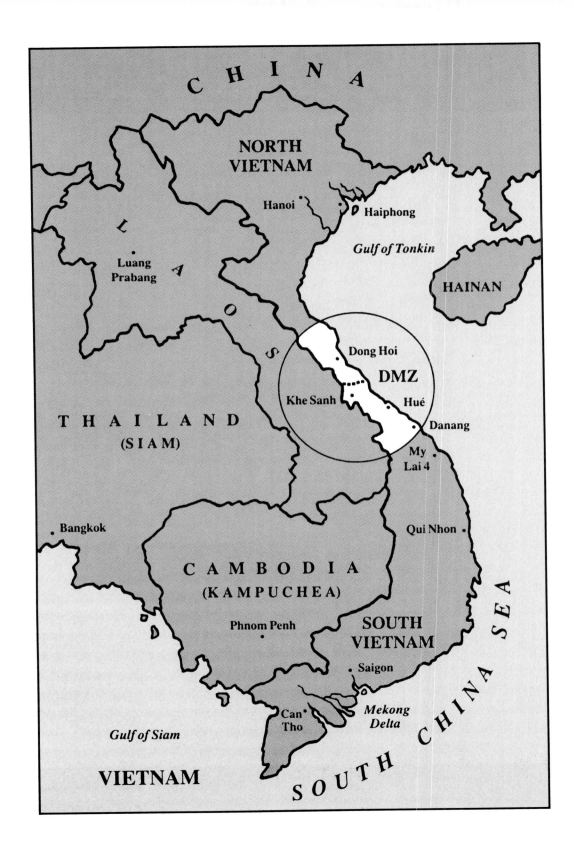

The Marines first heard of the Khe Sanh area in May 1967. Earlier in the war, the U.S. had established a small base in this beautiful, rolling valley and staffed it with Special Forces (Green Beret) advisers who worked with the Montagnard people. By mid-1967 thousands of North Vietnamese troops had moved into the area near Khe Sanh during the monsoon rains. They set up camps in the surrounding hills. When the first Marine troops arrived, the NVA soldiers were well dug in. Marine patrols paid with their lives for every foot of ground they walked. Their units advanced until they met solid enemy fire, then they dug in and called for air strikes to drop napalm and explosives on the enemy.

Savage fighting turned the jungle into bare, ripped earth, deeply pitted with bomb craters. Marine casualties during two weeks in May were reported at 1,000 dead and wounded. The North Vietnamese endured American bombing runs and retaliated by pounding the U.S. base camps with rockets, mortars, and artillery fire.

The Marines were forced to

Smoke from enemy rockets and mortars drifts over Khe Sanh.

defend hundreds of hills while under constant attack from enemy units that greatly outnumbered them. Their only hope for survival was air power and artillery, but these strikes did not always work. When a force of about 300 Marines was ambushed near Con Thien in July 1967, almost 100 Marines died in the fighting.

There seemed to be no clear-cut strategy behind the U.S. operations beyond hanging on to territory. A pattern was repeating itself in these grim battles that would become all too familiar throughout the rest of the war: the enemy acted and the U.S. reacted. Instead of having a plan and taking the initiative, American commanders waited for the VC and NVA to attack, then tried to wipe them out.

The North Vietnamese strategy seemed equally vague, however. Fighting in this remote part of South Vietnam was like trying to overrun the United States by capturing the Great Smokey Mountains. U.S. officials and military intelligence officers asked themselves what the North Vietnamese hoped to accomplish. Why seize territory that did not have much population? Why did they fight for a hill or valley, then abandon it as soon as the battle ended? Perhaps they intended to lure U.S. forces away from the cities, then attack the defenseless centers. Or was the enemy keeping score in the conflict by the number of Americans sent home in coffins?

By the end of 1967, the number of American dead was reaching disturbing proportions. The vast majority of U.S. deaths were among the Marines and Army personnel. The body of a soldier killed in combat usually was retrieved as soon as the battle ended. He was placed in an olive-colored plastic body bag and flown by helicopter to a main camp. A cargo plane or a truck then took the body to graves registration, which was located in an airplane hanger at Tan Son Nhut airbase outside Saigon. There the body was embalmed and put into a reusable aluminum coffin. As soon as a transport plane was filled with these coffins, it took off for the long flight to Oakland, California.

Before the body left Vietnam, the next of kin or family was notified. They were told by a mili-

U.S. Marine patrols took heavy casualties.

## Robert S. McNamara

*Robert S. McNamara (born June 9, 1916), U.S. Secretary of Defense, 1961-1968*

*A brilliant manager and organizer, McNamara served under both Kennedy and Johnson as America's Secretary of Defense. As was the case for many people close to the President at the time, Vietnam proved to be his downfall.*

*McNamara grew up in California and after graduating from college took a teaching assignment at Harvard University. He served in the Army Air Corps in World War II. When the war ended, he joined the Ford Motor Company, rising quickly through the ranks until he was named president in 1960. It was the same year John F. Kennedy won the presidential election.*

*Kennedy persuaded McNamara to join his cabinet as Secretary of Defense. The quiet, soft-spoken man quickly taught the armed forces to be more efficient. Because of his dedication and hard work, Johnson insisted that he stay on after Kennedy's death. Together they tried to achieve victory in Vietnam.*

*As Secretary of Defense, McNamara planned the U.S. buildup in Vietnam, despite his own misgivings about the war. Most of his information came from the South Vietnamese and military experts on the scene. McNamara became aware that many reports were exaggerated and in some cases invented. By 1966, however, there was no easy way for America to back out of the war. His efficient management of the Defense Department eventually broke down as the war got more and more out of control. He resigned in 1968 when Nixon was elected President.*

*McNamara had argued that helping Vietnam develop economically was as important as winning battles. He felt that the United States should help underdeveloped countries as much as possible. When he left the cabinet in 1968, he had an opportunity to put his beliefs into action. He was named president of the World Bank. By the time he retired in 1981, he had made over $13 billion in loans to poor countries. To this day, he avoids speaking about Vietnam in public.*

tary sergeant or officer who went to the home with the soldier's family priest, minister, or rabbi. The family also received telegrams confirming the death and telling them when they could expect the body. The officer

Inside a Khe Sanh bunker.

would then find out which funeral home was to receive the body. A soldier on the transport plane from Vietnam saw to it that the coffin got to the right funeral home. The same soldier would also tell the family if the dead man's remains could be viewed.

Soldiers killed in combat were usually awarded the Bronze Star medal with a tiny "V" pin on the ribbon, which stood for "valor." Soldiers who died in other ways were given a plain Bronze Star.

John Stolting, an Army staffer who worked in the 9th Infantry Division's awards and decorations office in 1967, recalls that about 30 percent of the deaths were caused by artillery fire from our own side, by drowning, or by accidents. On one occasion, Stolting was prepared to send Bronze Stars to four surviving families when an officer stopped him. "He said three of the guys should get Bronze Stars," Stolting remembers, "but the fourth guy didn't deserve one. He had been playing with a grenade as the four were riding in a helicopter. The grenade went off, killing all four men.''

Most Marines who died at Khe Sanh were killed by enemy artillery, rockets, and mortars. If the shrapnel did not get them, then they were killed when their own ammunition or fuel was hit and exploded. No buildings in Khe Sanh survived the daily and nightly pounding by the North Vietnamese. The 5,000 Marines dug their trenches and foxholes deeper and deeper as U.S. planes dropped nearly 6,000 tons of bombs on NVA positions each day. Each night the only letup in the firing came when the NVA crept up to and through strings of protective barbed wire around the camp. The Marines drove them back, then dug in as rockets and artillery exploded around them in the darkness.

Spotter planes showed that as many as 35,000 North Vietnamese surrounded Khe Sanh. The Marines had pushed them back into the DMZ in mid-1967, but they had found another route through Laos that took them back to Khe Sanh. This alternate route wound through jungle-covered valleys where the enemy was difficult to spot. They moved at night, sometimes walking in total darkness with a hand on the shoulder of the man in front of them. Once they reached the hills around Khe Sanh, they constructed fortified positions. Huge artillery pieces were brought in and hidden in the hills. These big guns could be fired, then quickly rolled back into caves and shelters. This technique prevented spotter planes from seeing the guns and calling bombers in to wipe them out.

As the fighting continued, Westmoreland committed more troops and air support to the battle. Winning this fight had become a top priority not only to the military but to President Johnson. They were haunted by the spectre of Dien Bien Phu in which the French had been surrounded and defeated by a superior Vietnamese force. President Johnson even had a model of Khe Sanh built so that he could follow the course of the battle. The American people were told that a decisive win in this region could mean a quicker end to the war. Pictures of the fighting in Khe Sanh became almost daily fare on television back in the United States.

Military advisers believed the battle was the first step in an NVA push to the South. As one Marine major said, "This is the cork, right here. If they get past us, they can tear up the countryside way over to the coast."

The Marines continued to send out patrols to scout enemy positions. No matter which direction they chose, they ran into enemy troops. When NVA forces outnumbered them, the Marines were usually overrun and wiped out. Occasionally, U.S. soldiers survived these fights to tell hair-raising stories. Two Marines, Corporal Steven Nelson of Elkhart, Indiana, and Lance Corporal Michael Roha, of National City, California, told of being captured northwest of Danang after their unit was overwhelmed. They were taken to a large bunker and held for several days. The two were able to escape by tiptoeing past a sleeping guard. They ran barefoot for seven miles through thick jungle to a Marine camp.

Not many prisoners were taken by the NVA or Viet Cong, because the enemy had no organized way to take care of them. Most soldiers and pilots who were cap-

Dieter Dengler before . . .

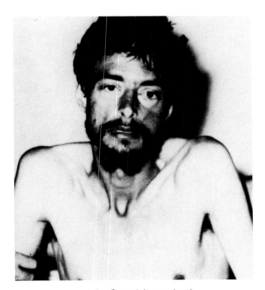

. . . and after his ordeal

A wounded American is carried to a helicopter.

tured were probably killed within a few days or sent to prison camps in the North. Only a few prisoners ever managed to get free. Deiter Dengler, a young jet pilot shot down over Laos in 1966, was the only flyer to escape during the entire war. Breaking away from his captors, he managed to survive 23 days in the Laotian jungle. Another soldier, Private First Class Roger Anderson, an infantryman, was captured near Can Tho in the Mekong Delta. He was held ten days before a U.S. helicopter fired on the boat where he was being held prisoner. He waved to the helicopter crew and was plucked from the muddy river water as his captors fled.

The Marines, surrounded at Khe Sanh, had no wish to become prisoners. They hung on grimly—putting up with the constant hammering of artillery, mortars, and rockets—and fought back. Numb from the battle, they sat in their foxholes in late January 1968 and wondered: What did the enemy have in mind? No one suspected that within a few days, the Viet Cong would launch the most massive attack of the war in South Vietnam.

# Chapter 8

# The Tet Offensive

In the night sky over Saigon, people were used to seeing distant flares, tracer bullets, searchlights, and even explosions from friendly and enemy rockets and mortars. The night of January 30-31, 1968, held another attraction. Brilliantly colored fireworks burst high above the city as more than two million people celebrated Tet, the start of the new year in many Far Eastern countries.

Tet, a week-long holiday, is Christmas, Easter, Fourth of July, and Mardi Gras all rolled into one. The celebration is marked by the purchase of new clothes, fancy food, and all types of candies. People visit friends and relatives, make resolutions to behave better, and hope for a prosperous life in the 12 months to come. Because it is such a special holiday, troops on both sides of the war usually observed a truce for two or more days. The year 1968 seemed no different.

South Vietnamese and U.S. officials felt they had reason to celebrate. Except for the fighting around Khe Sanh, recent reports seemed to indicate that at last the general tide of the war was turning in their favor. Viet Cong activities had been slowing down lately. Perhaps North Vietnam was growing weary of fighting. Perhaps the VC were running out of supplies and weapons to continue the war.

With tensions beginning to ease in Saigon, the two military policemen guarding the U.S. embassy in the city had no reason to expect trouble in the early morning hours of January 31. Charles E. Daniel and William E. Sebast, stationed at the only open gate to the embassy, watched idly as a taxicab and truck drove slowly past.

Suddenly the vehicles veered and headed straight for them. One of the passengers opened fire with a machine gun, and the bullets bounced off the embassy walls.

U.S. military police attempt to recapture the American embassy during the
1968 Tet Offensive.

The two policemen returned the fire and slammed the gate shut. They radioed for help as Viet Cong sappers (explosives experts) blew a gaping hole in the wall surrounding the embassy. The first two sappers through the hole were cut down by Daniel and Sebast; but within a short time the Americans were hit. Viet Cong fighters poured into the embassy grounds.

It was not an isolated attack. All over South Vietnam, cities and military bases were hit in a massive, coordinated assault. Hundreds of Viet Cong, armed with whatever weapons they could carry, attacked American and Vietnamese forces. Even Westmoreland's headquarters and the offices of the South Vietnamese military were shelled. U.S. and ARVN soldiers tumbled out of tents and bunkers everywhere to fight for their lives. Refugees in many cities, who might have forgotten the power of the Viet Cong, were given deadly reminders—VC rockets and mortars fired into refugee camps. The attacks were followed by Viet Cong fighters who entered the cities and towns to tell the people that a great uprising was under way throughout South Vietnam.

Within a few hours of the attack on the U.S. embassy, the whole world knew of the Tet Offensive. In the confusion, it was reported that the enemy had captured the main U.S. embassy building. Actually, three Marines and a handful of embassy employees kept the sappers between the building and the outer wall, despite rockets fired into the front door by the VC. U.S. and Vietnamese personnel from nearby buildings began shooting at the enemy, who were hiding behind large flower pots on the grounds. The VC fought for six hours before being killed or captured. Elsewhere, Viet Cong attacked the main radio station and rounded up and shot Saigon residents whom they knew backed the South Vietnamese government.

Radio transmitters were the targets of many VC sappers, and with good reason. The VC carried scripts with them to be read over the air to the South Vietnamese. They were going to tell soldiers to lay down their arms. Civilians would not be harmed if they cooperated.

Vietnamese civilians hide from the fighting in Saigon.

Although the VC failed to capture the radio stations, thousands of civilians were told by the enemy soldiers that this was the final battle. The bigger the city, the larger the enemy force attacking it. Thousands of Viet Cong around Saigon set up roadblocks on major highways, rocketed airports and military posts, and convinced frightened civilians that the end was near. More than half of South Vietnam's 14 million people were affected in some way by the Tet Offensive.

The assault came as a shock to the American people and the U.S. government. Everywhere people who supported the government said, "I thought we were winning the war." The military forces in Vietnam had no quick answers to give; they were too busy defending U.S. bases. In northern and central Vietnam, North Vietnamese Army units joined the Viet Cong attack. In and around Saigon and the Mekong Delta, the Tet Offensive was a VC operation.

As dawn broke on January 31, the fighting raged on. Tan Son Nhut airbase survived heavy rocket fire and a huge ground attack, thanks to the arrival of U.S. 25th Infantry Division troops. American soldiers from many units fought all over Saigon as helicopters and jet planes bombed enemy strongholds.

Newsfilm shot throughout the night and into the morning was rushed to Tan Son Nhut and put on a plane along with wounded soldiers headed for Japan. The film was flashed via satellite to network television. It showed incredible destruction, fierce fighting in and around the cities, helpless civilians fleeing the war zones, and weary, wounded young Americans. People across the country pushed aside their evening meals to watch the news. Parents and relatives of servicemen and women waited throughout the long hours of the battle, hoping that their loved ones had survived. General Westmoreland told reporters that 5,800 of the enemy had died in the first 24 hours. People in the U.S. wondered how many Americans lay dead in the wake of the offensive.

This massive, well-planned surprise attack had been developing for months. The Viet Cong had mingled with the civilian

Vietnamese firefighters braved heavy gunfire to put out blazes caused by the Tet Offensive.

## William C. Westmoreland

*William C. Westmoreland (born March 26, 1914), Army general and commander of U.S. forces in Vietnam, 1964-1968*

*Lean and handsome, William Westmoreland looked every inch the military general. He was born in South Carolina and graduated from West Point. His abilities quickly caught the eye of several high-ranking officers in the Army. One of those officers was General Maxwell Taylor, who would later serve as U.S. ambassador to South Vietnam.*

*Westmoreland was a war hero in World War II and Korea. He succeeded General Paul Harkins in Vietnam as head of America's military advisers. As more U.S. forces were sent to Vietnam, Westmoreland's role increased in importance. He influenced many of the decisions made by Johnson and his advisers. He favored bringing American fighting forces into Vietnam to take on the enemy and called repeatedly for bombing raids over North Vietnam. An astute military man, Westmoreland tried to keep military and political matters separate, but in Vietnam this proved hard to do.*

*Robert McNamara kept asking Westmoreland for figures from Vietnam that would tell him how the war was going. Westmoreland supplied the Secretary of Defense with enemy body count numbers drawn up by his own and South Vietnamese officers in the field. These figures were sometimes greatly exaggerated. When they were passed on to Washington, the reports gave a distorted picture of the real situation in Vietnam.*

*Years later, in 1982, a CBS television program accused Westmoreland of deliberately lying about the number of enemy troops in Vietnam at the start of the Tet Offensive. The general sued the network. The well-publicized case ended over two years later when CBS admitted it may have exaggerated some of the evidence against Westmoreland. However, there was evidence that he had misled the public on other aspects of the war. Westmoreland, having forced CBS to admit mistakes on its part, dropped his suit and did not press the matter further.*

A child clears debris after heavy fighting.

population in most cities and learned all they could about U.S. and South Vietnamese troop locations and strengths. Many Vietnamese working on U.S. bases were Viet Cong themselves or VC sympathizers. They gathered military intelligence and hid weapons, laid out their battle plans, and timed the moment of attack. VC troops who found themselves outnumbered or cut off from their main units fought stubbornly until they were nearly all killed. Others simply melted into a line of refugees or faded into a row of shacks or old French buildings. Snipers took up posts everywhere.

Television viewers saw terrible fighting in Cholon, the Chinese section of Saigon. Amid such familiar sights as a Shell gasoline station or a Coca-Cola truck, grenades exploded and machine gun fire ripped through buildings. Progress against the enemy by Americans and their allies seemed painfully slow. A wire service reported that the only stores open for business in Saigon belonged to the coffin makers.

Instead of jungle or mountain warfare, U.S. soldiers now found themselves fighting in Vietnam's

The U.S.S. *Pueblo* was seized by North Korea in January, 1968.

crowded cities. They were unable to call in air power or artillery because of the number of innocent men, women, and children all around them. The soldiers had to fight the enemy in an agonizing house-to-house battle.

The longest—and most difficult—fighting took place in the ancient capital of Hué. This city, with its centuries-old palace buildings, was overwhelmed by Viet Cong and NVA troops during the first day of Tet. While NVA soldiers held off American Marines and ARVN troops, the Viet Cong rounded up residents of the city. Many suspected of being government sympathizers were shot or buried alive. Civilians could find no safe place in Hué. The bitter fighting continued into late February before the VC and NVA forces were finally driven out of the city.

President Johnson, along with the rest of the country, watched the scenes unfold on his television screen. He told reporters the situation was under control. Privately the President had as many questions for his staff as he had answers for the press. How could they have underestimated the enemy so badly? His staff had no ready explanations.

Johnson believed that the Tet attack throughout South Vietnam was not simply a military venture. He reasoned that it was also an attempt on North Vietnam's part to influence U.S. public opinion against the war. Up to that time, a slim majority of the American people still believed that the U.S. was acting rightly and that the war could be won. If enough of them changed their minds, they might force a change in American policy and demand a withdrawal of American troops.

Johnson, an astute politician, had noticed throughout 1967 that peace protestors were attracting more average, middle-class Americans to their cause. His own supporters were either joining the antiwar movement themselves or being lured into the camp of Alabama Governor George Wallace or former Vice President Richard M. Nixon. Both these men were seeking the 1968 presidential nomination of their parties. With the presidential election only a few months off, the Tet Offensive hurt Johnson in many ways.

Even before the surprise enemy attack, however, Johnson had taken two actions that hurt his popularity. He called up 14,000 reserve soldiers to active duty after the North Koreans captured a U.S. ship, the *U.S.S. Pueblo.* He also asked Congress to raise taxes. The U.S. was spending more money than intended on the war, though LBJ bristled when Congressmen called the proposed tax a ''war levy.'' In truth, however, almost all of the $10.2 billion in additional revenue was earmarked for Vietnam.

Not until the fourth day of the Tet Offensive did the U.S. claim that Vietnam was once again under allied control, though fighting still raged at Hué. They had beaten back the enemy, but at an enormous cost. According to one writer, Don Oberdorfer, author of the book *Tet!*, the deaths alone were staggering. From January 29 to March 31, Oberdorfer records, the two sides suffered the following casualties:

- 3,895 American service personnel
- 214 allies (Australian, Korean, Thai, Filipino.)
- 4,954 South Vietnamese soldiers
- 58,000 Viet Cong and NVA troops
- 4,300 civilians

The destruction and loss of materiél were also immense. The airbase at Danang reported 5 aircraft destroyed and 37 planes and helicopters damaged. The monetary cost from that ground attack alone was $15 million. Elsewhere, years of American aid were wiped out in seconds as wells and dams were blown up, bridges destroyed, and rice bins emptied. Burned-out personnel carriers could be seen all along major roads. Bodies lay for days in the blazing sun and floated in the country's canals and rivers. The smell of death, destruction, and gunpowder hung over the countryside like a thick haze.

Recovery in some areas began long before the last enemy soldier was pulled from the wreckage of Hué. The daily briefings of reporters by the U.S. Public Affairs Office began again. Only now there were fewer reporters who believed the colonels and generals as they talked about "winning the hearts and minds" of the people. The briefings came to be known as the "Five o'Clock Follies."

Refugees clogged all the highways as country people headed toward the cities and city people fled from street fighting. Soldiers worked around the clock to rebuild bunkers and bases hit by rockets and to clear away debris from streets and runways.

Had they weathered the worst of it, they wondered, or was Tet only the beginning of things to come? How could the enemy keep coming back time after time? What would it take to beat them once and for all? Questions flew thick and fast. After five years of war and nearly 15,000 U.S. soldiers killed, the answers seemed as elusive as ever.

Tet fighting swelled the lines of refugees.

# Timeline of Vietnam: 3000 B.C. to 1988

**3000 B.C.** The people we call the Vietnamese begin to migrate south out of China.

**100 B.C.** Start of China's 1,000-year rule of Vietnam.

**A.D. 938** Vietnam becomes independent.

**1500** The first European explorers visit Vietnam.

**1640** Alexandre de Rhodes, a French Roman Catholic missionary, arrives in Vietnam.

**1744** Vietnam expands into the Mekong Delta. The Vietnamese by this date rule over all of present-day Vietnam.

**1844** The French fleet destroys Vietnam's navy.

**1859** Saigon falls to the French.

**1883** The French capture Hanoi.

**1930** Ho Chi Minh starts the Indochinese Communist Party.

**1939** The communist party is outlawed in Vietnam.

**1941** The Japanese take control of Vietnam as Ho Chi Minh returns from a Chinese prison and the Viet Minh (communist army) is founded.

**1945** Ho Chi Minh declares Vietnam independent as the Japanese surrender.

**1946** The French return, and the Viet Minh take to the hills as the French Indochina war begins.

**1952** Viet Minh forces are defeated several times by the French.

**1954** The French are defeated at Dien Bien Phu and agree to leave Vietnam. Vietnam is divided into north and south following a cease-fire agreed upon in Geneva, Switzerland.

**1955** The U.S. begins to send aid to South Vietnam.

**1956** President Ngo Dinh Diem refuses to hold elections, as had been promised in the Geneva agreement.

**1957** Communist guerrilla activities begin in South Vietnam.

**1959** The North Vietnamese start to send soldiers into South Vietnam.

**1963** The Viet Cong (South Vietnamese communists) defeat regular South Vietnamese soldiers at Ap Bac. This is the first major battle between the two sides. Buddhists protest South Vietnamese government policies. President Diem is overthrown and killed by the military.

**1964** A North Vietnamese patrol boat attacks an American destroyer in the Gulf of Tonkin. Congress gives President Lyndon B. Johnson special powers to act in Southeast Asia. The first American pilot is shot down and taken prisoner by the North Vietnamese.

### 1965

**1965** American air raids take place over North Vietnam. The first American combat troops arrive in South Vietnam.
**February 7** Viet Cong attack U.S. bases. President Johnson replies to the attacks by bombing targets in North Vietnam.

**March 8** The first American combat soldiers—3,500 Marines—arrive in Vietnam to guard Danang airbase.

**March 24** Antiwar teach-in is held at the University of Michigan, Ann Arbor, Michigan. Teach-ins take place throughout 1965 on many college and university campuses.

**April** North Vietnamese prepare the first launching pad for Russian surface-to-air (SAM) missiles.

**May 15** National antiwar teach-in held in Washington, D.C.

**May 24** First U.S. Army division leaves U.S. for Vietnam.

**June 11** Air Force General Nguyen Cao Ky takes over as South Vietnam's prime minister.

**July 28** General William Westmoreland, commander of American forces in Vietnam, asks for and gets an increase in U.S. troops.

**October through mid-November** U.S. Army soldiers defeat North Vietnamese Army (NVA) troops in the first major battle between American and North Vietnamese forces. The fighting takes place in the remote Ia Drang valley.

**December 25** U.S. bombing of North Vietnam is suspended by President Lyndon B. Johnson, who hopes the North Vietnamese will meet with him to talk peace.

**December 31** U.S. troop strength in Vietnam numbers 200,000.

### 1966

**January 31** President Johnson orders the bombing of North Vietnam to resume.

**January-February** The Senate Foreign Relations Committee questions President Johnson's advisers about U.S. involvement in the war.

**February 8** President Johnson and South Vietnamese leaders call for peace following a meeting in Hawaii.

**March 10** Buddhists demonstrate against the South Vietnamese government. Ky responds by using troops to quell demonstrations.

**April 12** B-52 bombers are used for the first time in bombing raids against North Vietnam.

**December** North Vietnamese leaders meet and agree to fight the war with both troops and diplomacy.

### 1967

**January** North Vietnam says that the U.S. must stop its air raids before peace talks can begin.

**January** Operation Cedar Falls begins. This massive military action is designed to rid the Iron Triangle near Saigon of enemy soldiers. Villages believed sympathetic to the Viet Cong are leveled and the people relocated to refugee camps.

**February 22** Operation Junction City begins. A plan to trap Viet Cong in a jungle area northwest of Saigon, the operation results in few VC captured despite five major battles.

**April 28** General William Westmoreland addresses Congress on the war in Vietnam, asking for greater support.

**July** The North Vietnamese meet to plan a "Great Uprising" in 1968 in the south. The uprising became known as the Tet Offensive.

**August** Secretary of Defense Robert McNamara meets behind closed doors with U.S. senators. He informs them the saturation bombing of North Vietnam is not weakening the North Vietnamese.

**September 3** General Nguyen Van Thieu is elected president of South Vietnam.

**November** U.S. Marines occupy Khe Sanh, a hilltop near the border of Laos. They are soon surrounded by over 35,000 NVA soldiers.

**December 31** The number of U.S. troops in Vietnam reaches nearly 500,000.

## 1968

**January 30-31** The Tet Offensive begins as Viet Cong and North Vietnamese troops attack most of the major cities in South Vietnam and the major American military bases.

**February 24** U.S. and South Vietnamese forces, after weeks of fighting, retake Hué, ending the Tet Offensive.

**March 10** *The New York Times* reports that General William Westmoreland wants 206,000 more American troops by the end of the year.

**March 12** Eugene McCarthy, the antiwar U.S. senator from Minnesota, receives 40 percent of the Democratic vote in the New Hampshire primary.

**March 16** Between 200 and 600 Vietnamese civilians are murdered by American troops in a village called My Lai 4.

**March 31** President Lyndon B. Johnson orders a halt to the bombing of North Vietnam and announces that he will not run again for the presidency.

**April 4** Dr. Martin Luther King, Jr., is shot to death in Memphis, Tennessee. Rioting erupts in many large U.S. cities.

**May 11** Formal peace talks begin in Paris between the United States and North Vietnam.

**June 6** U.S. Senator Robert Kennedy dies the day after he is shot in Los Angeles, California. Kennedy had been campaigning for the Democratic Presidential nomination.

**June 10** General Creighton Abrams takes command of U.S. forces in Vietnam.

**June 27** American troops leave Khe Sanh after several months of bitter fighting.

**July 1** U.S. planes resume bombing north of the DMZ.

**August 8** Richard M. Nixon is nominated by Republicans to run for the presidency.

**August 26-29** Vice President Hubert Humphrey is nominated for the presidency in Chicago as police and antiwar demonstrators clash violently in the city's streets.

**November 6** Richard M. Nixon is elected President.

**December 31** A total of 540,000 Americans are in Vietnam.

### 1969

**March 18** The secret bombing of Cambodia begins.

**March 28** U.S. and ARVN troops discover mass graves of civilians killed by Viet Cong and NVA during the Tet takeover of Hué.

**June 8** President Nixon announces that 25,000 American troops will be withdrawn, to be replaced by South Vietnamese forces.

**September 3** Ho Chi Minh dies in Hanoi at the age of 79.

**Fall** Huge antiwar rallies take place in Washington, D.C.

**November 16** The country learns of the My Lai 4 massacre.

**December 31** The number of U.S. troops in South Vietnam drops to 480,000.

### 1970

**February 20** Henry Kissinger and Le Duc Tho of North Vietnam meet secretly in Paris.

**March 18** Prince Sihanouk of Cambodia is overthrown.

**April 30** American and South Vietnamese forces invade Cambodia.

**May 4** National Guardsmen kill 4 antiwar students and wound 11 others at Kent State University in Ohio.

**December 31** The number of U.S. troops in Vietnam falls to 280,000.

### 1971

**January 6** Congress repeals the Gulf of Tonkin Resolution.

**February 8** South Vietnamese forces enter Laos in an attempt to cut the Ho Chi Minh trail.

**March 29** Lieutenant William Calley is convicted of murder in connection with the massacre at My Lai 4.

**December 31** U.S. forces now total 140,000.

### 1972

**May 8** President Nixon orders the mining of Haiphong harbor and steps up the bombing.

**June 17** A night watchman catches five men attempting to break into Democratic national headquarters at the Watergate apartment-hotel complex in Washington, D.C.

**November 7** Richard Nixon is re-elected President.

**December 31** U.S. combat troops number fewer than 30,000.

### 1973

**January 27** An agreement is reached between the United States and North Vietnam to end the war in South Vietnam.

**March 29** The last U.S. troops leave South Vietnam. The only Americans left behind are 8,500 civilians, plus embassy guards and a small number of soldiers in a defense office.

**April 5** The U.S. Senate votes 88-3 to forbid aid to Vietnam without congressional approval.

**August 15** The bombing of Cambodia by American planes ends. President Nixon criticizes Congress for ending the air war.

**October 16** Henry Kissinger and Le Duc Tho are awarded the Nobel Peace Prize for ending the war in Indochina. Tho turns down the award because, as he points out, fighting continues.

## 1974

**April 4** The U.S. House of Representatives rejects a White House proposal for more aid to South Vietnam.

**August 9** Richard M. Nixon resigns as President of the United States and thus stops impeachment proceedings. Vice President Gerald Ford is sworn in as President.

## 1975

**January 6** The province of Phuoc Long, only 60 miles north of Saigon, is captured by the communists.

**March 14** President Nguyen Van Thieu decides to pull his troops out of the central highlands and northern provinces.

**April 8** A huge U.S. cargo plane, loaded with Vietnamese orphans, crashes on takeoff near Saigon. More than 100 children die.

**April 17** Cambodia falls to the Khmer Rouge (Cambodian communists).

**April 30** Saigon falls to the Vietnamese communists.

**December 3** Laos falls to the Pathet Lao (Laotian communists).

## 1976

**July 2** The two Vietnams are officially reunified.

**November 2** James Earl (Jimmy) Carter is elected President of the United States.

## 1977

**January 21** President Carter pardons 10,000 draft evaders. Throughout the year more and more refugees (''boat people'') leave Vietnam by any means available. Many are ethnic Chinese who fear persecution from Vietnamese victors.

## 1978

**December** Vietnamese forces occupy Cambodia.

## 1979

**February 17** China invades Vietnam and is in the country for three weeks.

**November 24** The U.S General Accounting Office indicates that thousands of Vietnam veterans were exposed to the herbicide known as Agent Orange. The veterans claim they have suffered physical and psychological damage from the exposure.

## 1980

**Summer** Vietnamese army pursues Cambodians into Thailand.

**November 4** Ronald Reagan is elected President of the United States.

## 1982

**November 13** The Vietnam Veterans' Memorial is dedicated in Washington, D.C.

## 1984

**May 7** Seven U.S. chemical companies agree to an out-of-court settlement with Vietnam veterans over manufacture of the herbicide Agent Orange. The settlement is for $180 million.

**July 15** Major fighting breaks out along the Vietnam-China border.

## 1986

**December** Vietnam's aging leaders step down after failing to improve the economy.

## 1988

**June** Vietnamese troops begin to withdraw from Cambodia.

# Glossary

The glossary of each book in this series introduces various Vietnamese and American terms used throughout the war.

**AK-47**: The standard rifle carried by the North Vietnamese Army. Lightweight and automatic, this Russian weapon was copied by the Chinese and renamed Type 56.

**Bunker**: A protected area where troops can shoot or hide from enemy fire. U.S. bunkers usually were made of sandbags. Enemy bunkers were constructed of fallen trees or earth. Both sides also dug trenches and foxholes for protection.

**Cadre**: A French word meaning *the middle*, around which an organization could be built. In South Vietnamese villages, the cadre was one or more Viet Cong who lived with villagers, gained their confidence and support, and turned them against the South Vietnamese government and their American allies.

*Chieu hoi*: A Vietnamese phrase meaning "open arms." Chieu hoi was a plan to make it easy for Viet Cong guerrillas to surrender and start a new life. The program failed to attract many VC, despite promises of job training and money.

**Cholon**: The part of Saigon where people of Chinese descent lived. This area was the scene of heavy fighting during the 1968 Tet Offensive.

**Conscientious objector**: A person whose religious or philosophical beliefs do not allow him to take part in combat. Many young men during the Vietnam War years served in noncombat jobs because they were conscientious objectors.

**Dove**: Any American who was against the U.S. military involvement in Vietnam. The term comes from the symbolic bird of peace. Prominent doves included J. William Fulbright, actress Jane Fonda, Dr. Benjamin Spock, and many students, faculty, and religious and lay leaders.

**Enclave or fortress strategy**: A plan devised when American troops first came to Vietnam in which they would simply defend bases or enclaves. The plan failed because South Vietnamese troops needed help fighting the Viet Cong and North Vietnamese Army. The enclave strategy was abandoned in favor of large-scale operations.

**Hawk**: Any American who supported the U.S. military involvement in Vietnam. The term comes from the bird of prey. Hawks included Secretary of State Dean Rusk, comedian Bob Hope, actor John Wayne, and many business and military leaders.

**Hoi chanh**: A Vietnamese term referring to an enemy who surrenders under the *chieu hoi* or "open arms" program. *Hoi chanh* were promised money and a new life if they came over to the South Vietnamese side.

**Howitzer**: A short cannon that fires exploding shells for several miles.

**Landing zone (LZ)**: A clearing where helicopters land so that troops can jump out. A "hot" LZ means that there is enemy fire all around the landing zone.

**Light antitank weapon (LAW)**: This device is a disposable fiberglass tube with a sight and firing mechanism that fires a shell straight ahead. It is held on the shoulder, like a World War II bazooka. The LAW was used by U.S. troops against fortified enemy bunkers.

**M-16 rifle**: The rifle carried by American soldiers in Vietnam. Weighing only six pounds, the weapon can be fired on single shot or automatic. After it was redesigned by U.S. defense technicians, the weapon began to jam and prove otherwise unreliable because of the mud, heat, and heavy use in Vietnam.

**M-79 weapon**: A shotgun-like U.S. weapon that fires a grenade much farther than a human arm can throw it. Excellent for use in the open, the weapon was limited in the jungle, where the shell sometimes hit trees or vines before reaching its target.

**Mortar**: A device made up of a tube, a base, and tripod-type legs. A small artillery shell is dropped down the tube, hits the base, and is fired into the air. The weapon can be set up or taken apart quickly and was used extensively by both sides.

**Sapper**: A Viet Cong commando trained to infiltrate U.S. or South Vietnamese positions. Sappers usually were experts in using explosives.

**Shrapnel**: Hot, jagged metal produced when a grenade or any kind of mortar or artillery shell explodes. Shrapnel was the most common cause of wounds among soldiers and civilians in Vietnam.

**Students for a Democratic Society (SDS):** An organization founded by students in the early 1960s. SDS took the lead in the antiwar movement on many college campuses, but never had more than 25,000 members. The association gradually broke apart over issues such as violent versus nonviolent protests.

**Surface-to-air missile (SAM):** Russian-made missiles used throughout the war by the North Vietnamese against U.S. planes. SAMs were guided by radio transmitters.

**Vietnam Veterans Against the WAR (VVAW):** A loosely organized group of veterans who worked to aid Vietnam veterans and demonstrated for peace in Vietnam. Though they never numbered more than 7,000, the organization showed that some of those who had served in the war were opposed to it.

An infantryman guides the landing of a U.S. helicopter.

# Index

# Index

Air Force jets swoop low in a bombing run over Vietnamese jungle.

# Acknowledgments

The series *War in Vietnam* is the product of many talented and dedicated people. Their stories, experiences, and skills helped make this series a unique contribution to our knowledge of the Vietnam era.

Author David K. Wright would like to thank the following people for their assistance: Yen Do, former Saigon resident and now a newspaper publisher in California; David Doyle, who works with resettled Hmong people from Laos; John Kuehl and Don Luce, both employees of Asia Resource Center in Washington, D. C.; Patricia (Kit) Norland of the Indochina Project in Washington, D. C.; John Stolting, 9th Infantry Division, Awards and Decorations section; and Frank Tatu, Don Ehlke, and Donald Wright, all veterans of the Vietnam War. These individuals gave generously of their time in personal interviews and provided resources on Southeast Asian history and current conditions.

A special thanks to Frank Burdick, Professor of History at State University College in Cortland, New York. Professor Burdick reviewed the manuscripts and made many valuable suggestions to improve them.

The editorial staff at Childrens Press who produced the four books of this series include Fran Dyra, Vice President, Editorial; Margrit Fiddle, Creative Director; L. Sue Baugh, Project Editor; Judy Feldman, Photo Editor; and Pat Stahl and Norman Zuefle, Editorial Proofreaders. Charles Hills of New Horizons & Associates created the dramatic book design for the series.

# Picture Acknowledgments

The Bettmann Archive—11, 15, 22, 23, 40-41, 45, 46, 57, 61, 62, 63, 66, 68-69, 72, 76, 79, 83, 85, 90, 92, 96-97, 110-111, 115, 140-141

Black Star:

© Wang Tzi—Front Cover

© Paul Avery/Empire News—2-3

© Richard Lawrence Stack—24-25

© James Pickerell—32

© Francois Scully—54-55

© Owen—70, 73, 80-81

© AGIP—93

© Robert Ellison—107

© Claus C. Meyer—118

© David Terry—123

Wide World Photos, Inc.—4-5, 8, 9, 10, 12, 16, 17, 20-21, 27, 31, 35, 36, 37, 39, 42, 47, 49, 51, 53, 58, 60, 65, 74-75, 77, 86, 89, 91, 94, 98, 102-103, 104, 106, 109-both images, 113, 116, 119, 120, 134, Back Cover

Maps—18, 19, 29, 30, 101

# About the Author

David K. Wright is a freelance writer who lives in Wisconsin. He grew up in and around Richmond, Indiana, and graduated from Wittenberg University in Springfield, Ohio, in 1966.

Wright received his draft notice the day after he graduated from college. He was inducted in September 1966 and arrived in Vietnam at Bien Hoa in March 1967. He served in the U.S. Army 9th Infantry Division as an armor crewman. Wright was stationed at Camp Bearcat, east of Saigon, and at Dong Tam in the Mekong Delta. He returned from Vietnam in March 1968 and was honorably discharged in September of that year, having attained the rank of Specialist five.

This is the second in a series of four books by Wright for Childrens Press about the Vietnam War. He also has written a book on Vietnam and a book on Malaysia in the *Enchantment of the World* series also published by Childrens Press.